Visual Reference Basics

Microsoft® Excel® 97

Karl Schwartz

Acknowledgements

Technical Editor
Cathy Vesecky

Layout and Design
Karl Schwartz

Copyright 1997 by DDC Publishing, Inc.

Published by DDC Publishing, Inc.

10 9 8 7 6 5

Printed in the United States of America.

Introduction

DDC's *Visual Reference Basics* series is designed to help you make the most of your Microsoft software. Newly updated to reflect changes and enhancements in Microsoft 97 applications, the *Visual Reference Basics* are equally useful as instruction manuals or as desktop reference guides for the experienced user. With illustrations and clear explanations of every step involved, they make even complex processes easy to understand and follow.

The most distinctive feature of this series is its extensive use of visuals. Buttons, toolbars, screens, and commands are all illustrated so that there is never any doubt that you are performing the right actions. Most information can be understood at a glance, without a lot of reading through dense and complicated instructions. With *Visual Reference Basics*, you learn what you need to know quickly and easily.

This book contains one hundred functions essential for optimal use of Microsoft Excel 97. These functions are arranged for ease of use. Cross-references in chapters help you to find related topics. Notes on each page give additional information or tips to supplement the directions given. The only thing *you* need to get the most out of the *Visual Reference Basics* series is a basic understanding of Windows and the desire to become more familiar with Excel.

The *Visual Reference Basics* series is an informative and convenient way to acquaint yourself with the capabilities of your Microsoft application. It is a valuable resource for anyone who wants to become a power user of Microsoft 97 software.

Table of Contents

Getting Started

Basic Skills

Formulas, Lists and Data Tables

Printing and Page Setup

Charts

Getting Started

This section contains essential information for new users of Microsoft Excel 97. Topics, in this section only, are listed in a logical order beginning with **Start Excel**.

Start Excel

When you start Excel, Windows copies the program into memory, and Excel automatically opens a blank workbook named Book1. You can start Excel in a variety of ways.

Start Excel Using Start Menu

1 Click **Start** button on Windows toolbar.

2 Point to **Programs** on **Start** menu.

A submenu appears.

3 Click **Microsoft Excel** icon.

The Excel application starts and opens a blank workbook named Book1.

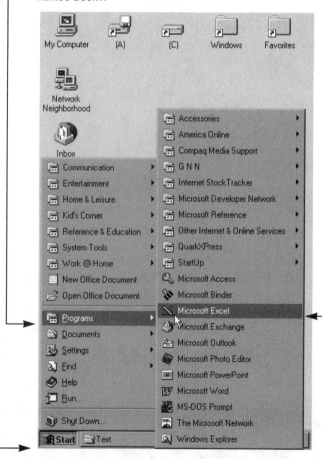

The Start Menu

2

- The **Office Shortcut Bar** may appear in a different location on your desktop. If it is not installed, you can add it by running Office setup.

- In the **New Office Document** dialog box, you can click the **Spreadsheet Solutions** tab to open Excel templates, instead of starting a new document from scratch.

- You can also start Excel by opening a recently used Excel document. Click the **Start** menu, point to **Documents**, and click the desired Excel document from the menu.

Start Excel from Microsoft Office

This method requires that Excel be installed as part of Microsoft Office 97.

1 Click the **Start** button on the Windows toolbar, then click **New Office Document** on the **Start** menu.

OR

If the **Office Shortcut Bar** is installed and running, click the **New Office Document** button on the Shortcut bar.

2 From the **General** tab, double-click the **Blank Workbook** icon.

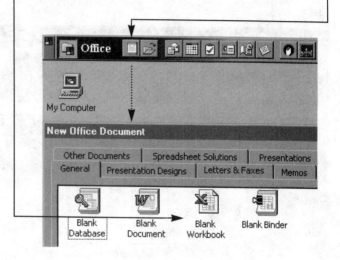

New Office Document Dialog Box

TIP: You can double-click any Excel document from a Windows folder to start Excel and open that file. If Excel is already running, just the file opens.

About the Excel Window

Excel provides an interface (graphical tools and controls) for working with worksheet data. This topic will help you to identify the purpose of the tools and indicators that appear in the Excel window.

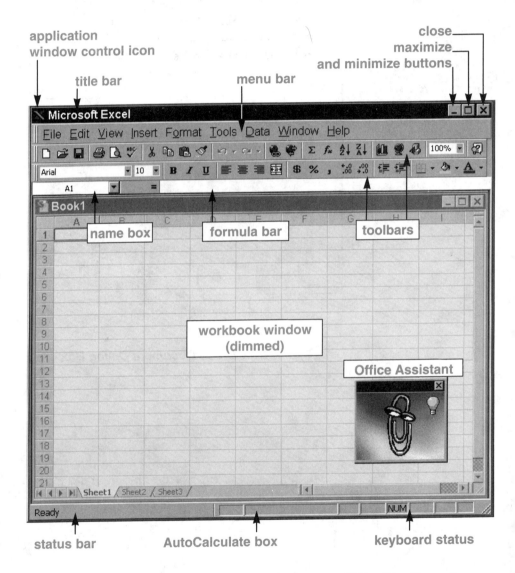

The Excel 97 Application as It Appears When You Open It

- In the illustration, there are two sets of **close**, **maximize** and **minimize** buttons: One for the Excel application window, and one for the workbook window. The **maximize** button will appear as a **restore** button if the window has already been maximized.

- If the workbook was maximized in the illustration, its name (Book1) would appear in the Excel application title bar, and the workbook title bar would not be available. *(See Window Controls for information about maximizing and restoring windows.)*

The Microsoft Excel Window

Microsoft Excel title bar: Displays the program name (Microsoft Excel), and may also display the file name of an open workbook window, if the workbook is maximized. You can drag the title bar to move the window, or double-click it to maximize the window.

Application window control icon: Click it to access a drop-down menu of commands that control the position and size of the application window.

Close, maximize, and minimize buttons: Click buttons to close, maximize, or minimize the Excel window. *(See Use Window Controls.)*

Menu bar: Displays menu names which, when clicked, display drop-down menus. *(See About Commands.)*

Toolbars: Click buttons on toolbar to select commands quickly, without opening a menu or dialog box. *(See About Toolbars.)*

Name box: Displays the cell reference of the active cell. *(See About Cells.)*

Formula bar: Provides a space for typing or editing cell data. *(See Edit Cells.)*

Status bar: Displays information about the current mode, selected command, or option. The right side of the status bar shows the **keyboard status**. For example, NUM indicates the numeric keyboard is active (number lock). The middle of the status bar contains the **AutoCalculate box**, which displays the result of a selected AutoCalculate function (such as SUM or AVERAGE) when applied to a selected range of cells. *(See AutoCalculate.)*

Office Assistant: Appears when you open Excel, and can answer your questions about how to perform a task. *(See Use Help.)*

Workbook window: Appears in, and is restricted to, the Excel window. Workbook windows contain the data that you enter in worksheets (purposely muted in this illustration). You can open multiple workbook windows within Excel. *(See About Workbooks.)*

About Workbooks

A workbook is a file in which you store and analyze information. Each workbook may contain multiple worksheets (sheets). This lets you organize related information in one workbook file. Workbooks are generally given descriptive names and are stored and retrieved from folders on a disk.

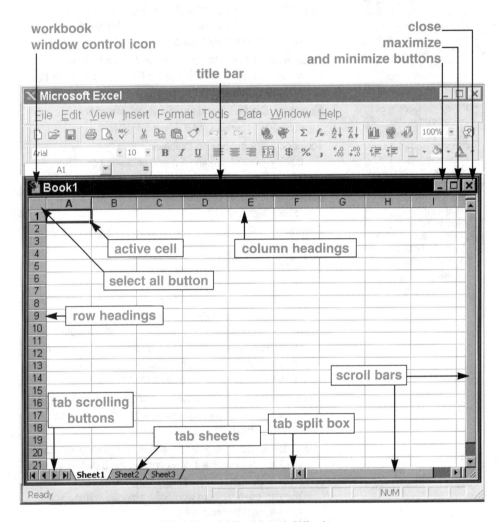

workbook
window control icon

close

maximize
and minimize buttons

title bar

active cell

column headings

select all button

row headings

scroll bars

tab scrolling
buttons

tab split box

tab sheets

The Excel Workbook Window

The Workbook Window

- In the illustration, there are two sets of **close**, **maximize** and **minimize** buttons: One for the Excel application window, and one for the workbook window. The **maximize** button will appear as a **restore** button if the window has already been maximized.

- If the workbook was maximized in the illustration, its name (Book1) would appear in the Excel application title bar, and the workbook title bar would not be available. *(See Window Controls for information about maximizing and restoring windows.)*

Workbook (Book1): Displays the active worksheet (Sheet1). It is the document window that opens when you start Excel. By default, workbooks contain three worksheets (Sheet1 – Sheet3), but can hold up to 255 sheets, which you can use to store data and formulas, charts, or macros.

Workbook window title bar: Displays the workbook file name. You can drag the title bar to move the window or double-click it to maximize the window size. A maximized workbook window does not have a title bar. Its file name appears on Excel's application window title bar.

Workbook control menu icon: Click the workbook window control menu box to access commands that control the workbook window. If the workbook window is maximized, its control menu icon is located on the left side of the Excel window menu bar. The workbook window **close**, **maximize**, and **minimize** buttons let you control the size, minimize, or close the Excel window. *(See Use Window Controls.)*

Row and column headings: Defines a cell's location and lets you adjust row and column dimensions with the mouse. Rows are numbered, and columns are lettered. *(See Adjust and Hide Columns/Rows.)*

Active cell: When a cell is active, you can type data into it. The active cell has a dark outline (i.e., cell A1 in the illustration on the previous page). *(See About Cells.)*

Select all button: Click it to select all the cells in the worksheet. *(See Select Cells.)*

Tab scrolling buttons: Click buttons to scroll to sheet tabs that are not in view. *(See Sheet Tabs.)*

Sheet tabs: Indicate the names of worksheets, charts, and modules in the workbook. Click a sheet tab to display that sheet in the workbook window. The active sheet tab is shown in bold (i.e., Sheet1 in the illustration on the previous page). *(See Sheet Tabs.)*

Tab split box: Drag to the right to display more sheet tabs or to the left to show more of the horizontal scroll bar. *(See Sheet Tabs.)*

Scroll bars: Use to display areas of the worksheet that are not in view. *(See Use Window Controls.)*

About Worksheets and Sheet Tabs

By default, each new workbook contains three worksheets labeled Sheet1 through Sheet3, illustrated below. Also see *Sheet Tabs* for information about inserting, grouping, renaming, deleting, moving, and copying sheet tabs.

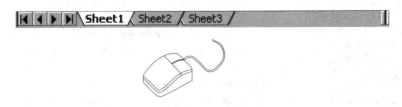

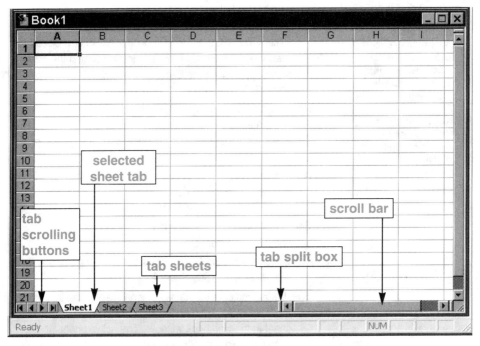

Workbook Sheet Tabs and Controls

Notes:

- A workbook holds up to 255 sheets displaying your data and formulas, charts, or macros. Macros are stored on module sheets; charts are stored on Chart sheets.

- To change the number of sheets in a new workbook, click the **Tools** menu, then **Options**, select the **General** tab, and set the number in **Sheets in new workbook** spin box.

- You can select (group) multiple sheets by pressing **Ctrl** and clicking the desired sheets. This lets you format or enter identical data in multiple worksheets in one step. *(See Sheet Tabs.)*

- Each sheet maintains its own settings, such as zoom, active cell, page margins, and gridlines.

- If a sheet is hidden, it will not appear as a sheet tab. *(See Hide and Unhide Sheets.)*

Worksheet Tab Controls

Tab scrolling buttons: Click to scroll to sheet tabs that are not in view.

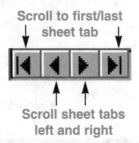

Scroll to first/last sheet tab

Scroll sheet tabs left and right

Sheet tabs: Indicate the names of worksheets, charts, and modules in the workbook. Click a sheet tab to display the sheet in the workbook window. The active sheet tab is shown in bold (i.e., Sheet1 in the illustration on the previous page). You can insert, delete, move, and rename sheet tabs. *(See Sheet Tabs.)*

Tab split box: Drag to the right to display more sheet tabs or to the left to show more of the horizontal scroll bar. To drag the tab split box, rest your mouse pointer on the tab split box control. (Note that the mouse pointer changes to a left and right facing arrow as shown below.) Then drag the split box left or right.

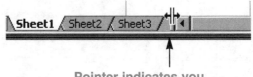

Pointer indicates you can drag split box

Scroll bars: Use to display areas of the active worksheet that are not in view. *(See Use Window Controls.)*

Use Window Controls

Window controls are graphical elements such as window borders, title bars, and close buttons that you can use to control the size or position of the Excel and workbook windows.

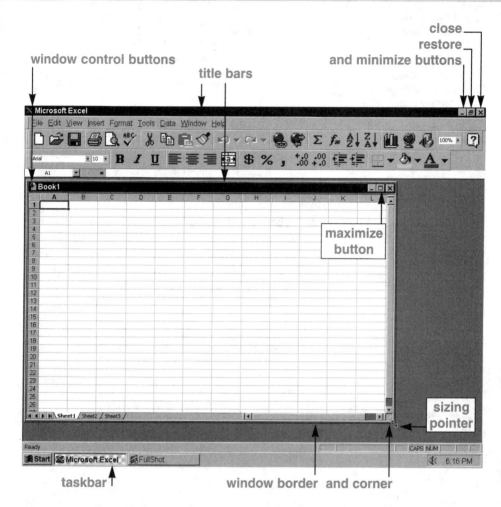

Excel Window Maximized, Workbook Not Maximized

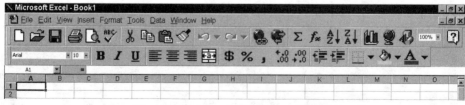

Excel and Workbook Windows Maximized

10

- In the top example: The Excel window contains close, *restore*, and minimize buttons, while the workbook window contains close, *maximize*, and minimize buttons. Unlike the maximized Excel window, you can size and move the workbook window because it has not been maximized.

- In the lower example: Both windows have been maximized. The workbook's minimize, restore, and close buttons appear on the Excel menu bar. You cannot size or move either window. Notice the workbook window does not have a title bar, and its name (Book1) appears in the Excel title bar.

Window Controls

Close button: Click it to close the Excel or workbook window. You will be prompted to save changes to the workbook if you have not already done so.

Maximize button: Click it to enlarge the window to fill the screen, or, for a workbook, to fill the Excel window.

Minimize button: In the Excel window, click it to reduce the window to a button on the taskbar. In workbook windows, click it to reduce the window to a button within the Excel application window.

Restore button: Click it to restore a maximized window to its previous size.

Sizing pointer: The mouse pointer becomes a sizing pointer when you rest it on a window border or corner. This indicates that you can change the border by dragging it.

Taskbar: Click buttons on it to select a window that is not in view (hidden behind other windows), or to open a window you have minimized.

Title bar: Drag it to move a window, or double-click it to maximize/restore the window. Maximized windows cannot be moved or sized.

Window border or corner: Drag it to change the size of the window. The pointer becomes a sizing pointer when positioned on a window border or corner.

Window control buttons: Click to open a menu of commands that control the window, e.g., Restore, Minimize, and Close. You can open this menu with the keyboard:

Excel window   press **Alt+Space**
Workbook window   press **Alt+-** (hyphen)

About Commands

Commands allow you to tell Excel what actions to take. For example, when you want to save the current workbook, you will execute the File, Save command. This topic will show you how to use the menu bar, shortcut menus, and keystrokes to execute commands.

File Edit View Insert Format Tools Data Window Help

Choose Menu Commands

1 If required, select cells or object the command will apply to.

2 Click desired menu name on menu bar.
   Excel opens a drop-down menu.

3 Click the desired menu command.

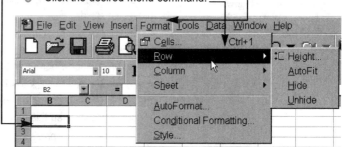

Format Menu Commands

12

Shortcut Menu Commands

1 Rest pointer on selected cell or object.
2 Right-click selected cell or object.
 Excel opens a context-sensitive menu.
3 Click the desired menu command.

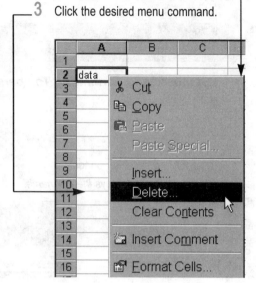

Keyboard Commands

1 Select cell or object to which command will apply.
2 Press desired command key, such as **Ctrl+X** (Cut).
 Excel performs the action.

TIP: When you click a name on a menu, Excel displays keyboard commands next to many command options.

About Toolbars

Excel displays the Standard and Formatting toolbars, by default. These toolbars contain buttons that let you execute commands quickly, without opening menus and dialog boxes. As you work, Excel will display other toolbars for special tasks, such as editing a chart.

Standard and Formatting Toolbars

Notes:

- Excel may display additional information with the button name. For example, it will show the name of the current printer when you rest the pointer on the **Print** button.

Show Purpose of Toolbar Button

- Rest pointer on tool.
  Excel displays the tool name.

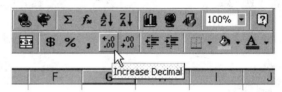

Notes:

- If you select a cell that has been bolded, the **Bold** button on the toolbar will invert to indicate that setting has been applied. Most buttons work this way, except the **Borders**, **Fill Color**, and **Font Color** buttons, which show the last attribute applied to any cell – not the current setting.

Use a Toolbar Button

1 Select cells or object the command will apply to.

2 Click appropriate button on toolbar.

If the button contains a drop-down arrow:

a Click the arrow to open the list or palette.

b Click the appropriate item in the list or palette.

OR

- Click the icon to the left of the drop-down arrow to apply the current setting for the tool.

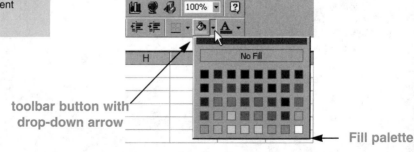

toolbar button with drop-down arrow

Fill palette

14

- In **step 1**, to right-click an item, point to the item, then press and release the right mouse button.

- In **step 2**, if the toolbar is already showing, a check mark appears to the left of the toolbar name.

- The **Customize** option lets you add and remove buttons on existing toolbars or create new toolbars to meet your special needs. You can also change the size of toolbar buttons and enable or disable ScreenTips on toolbars by selecting these options on the **Options** tab of the **Customize** dialog box.

Show or Hide a Toolbar

1 Right-click any area of any toolbar.
   Excel displays a list of available toolbars.
2 Click the desired toolbar to hide or show it.

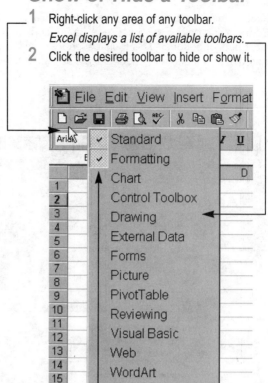

active toolbars have checks

- Toolbars that have been moved from their docked positions are called **floating toolbars**.

- In **step 2**, when you drag a toolbar away from its docked position, a title bar appears on it, indicating it has become a floating toolbar.

Move a Toolbar

1 Point to a blank area of toolbar you want to move.
   OR
   Point to title bar of floating toolbar.
2 Drag toolbar to desired position in Excel window.

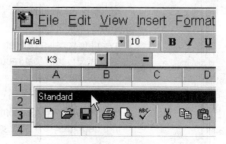

Floating Toolbar

Use Dialog Box Controls

When you select certain commands, Excel will open a dialog box displaying sets of related options. Some dialog boxes, such as Page Setup, contain tabs that you can click to display additional sets of options. This topic describes how to use the controls in a dialog box, such as option buttons and check boxes, so you can work efficiently with Excel.

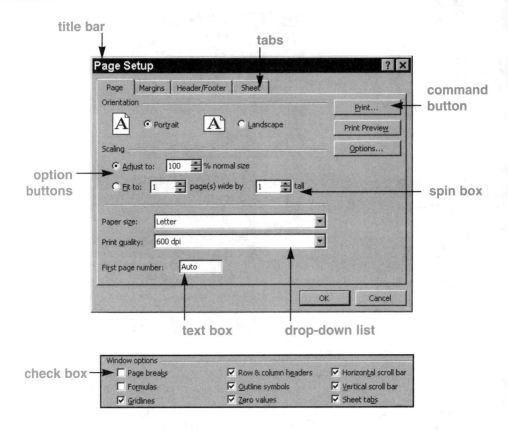

Dialog Box Controls

A dialog box contains different ways to ask you for information:

Title bar: Identifies the title of the dialog box, which is Page Setup in the illustration.

Text box: Click in the box, then type information. Text boxes meant to receive cell references have collapse buttons (see next page) that reduce the dialog box to allow a better view of the worksheet.

Command buttons: Click to carry out actions described by the button name. When command names have ellipses following them, they will access another dialog box.

Drop-down list: Click the drop-down list arrow to open a short list of options. Make a choice from the options provided.

Spin box (or increment box): Type a value in the box, or click the up or down arrow (usually to the right of the box) to select a value.

Tab: Displays related options in the same dialog box. Click a tab to access its options.

Option buttons: Click to select one option appearing in a set of options. A selected option button contains a dark circle.

Check box: Click to select or deselect an option. A check mark in the box indicates the option is selected.

Notes:

- In a dialog box you may want to insert a cell reference to define a print area, for example. Excel 97 provides a collapse button that reduces the size of the dialog box, so that you can see the worksheet and select the reference instead of typing it.

Use Dialog Collapse Buttons to Insert Cell References

1 Click the **collapse** button.

The dialog box collapses.

2 Drag through cells to define the cell reference.

3 Click the **expand** button when done.

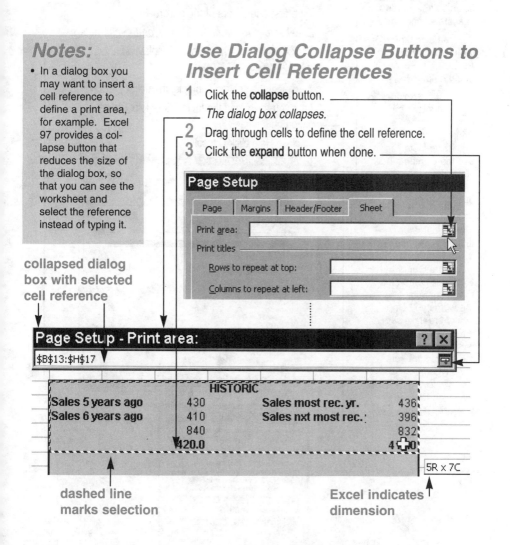

collapsed dialog box with selected cell reference

dashed line marks selection

Excel indicates dimension

Use Help

When you need to learn how to perform a task, Excel's online Help system is always just a few clicks away. Excel provides help in many dialog boxes. Additionally, the Office Assistant will automatically suggest better ways to do your work.

Help ➡ ? Microsoft Excel Help / 📖 Contents and Index

Notes:

- The **Index** tab contains an extensive list of items organized by key words in alphabetical order.

- You can also use the tools on the remaining Help tabs to get help.

Contents: Provides help organized by topics, such as Printing and Managing Lists. To use the Contents Help, double-click the desired topic to open subtopics.

Find: Creates a search index the first time you open it. You can then type words, and Excel will search for topics containing all the words you type in any order. A second box displays the words that match the characters you have typed. A third box displays the matching topics that you can display.

Search Index for Help

1 Click **Help** menu, then click **Contents and Index**.

2 Click the **Index** tab.

3 Type first characters of topic word.

   Excel scrolls to the item as you type the characters.

4 Click desired topic, then click **Display**.

   If a subtopic window opens:

   • Select the desired subtopic, then click **Display**.

5 After you have read the topic, click **Help Topics** button on toolbar.

6 To close Help click **Cancel**.

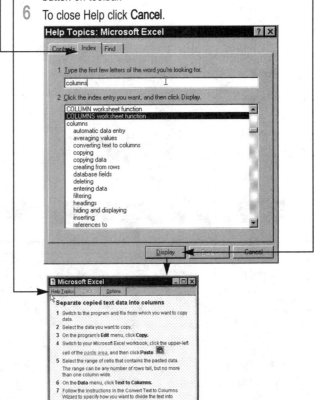

Notes:

- In **step 2**, you can click any option or dialog box control, such as a toolbar or command button.

Get Help in a Dialog Box

1 Click **Help** button on dialog box title bar.

A ? appears next to pointer.

2 Click the option you want help on.

Excel displays help for the clicked option.

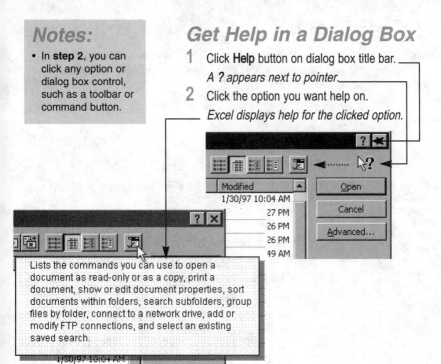

Notes:

- If Office Assistant is not available, click the **Office Assistant** button on the Standard toolbar.

Get Help from Office Assistant

1 Click the **Office Assistant** button on the Standard toolbar.

OR

Click anywhere on the Office Assistant.

2 Type your question in the text box and click **Search**.

3 Click the button next to the desired topic.

4 Click **Close** when done.

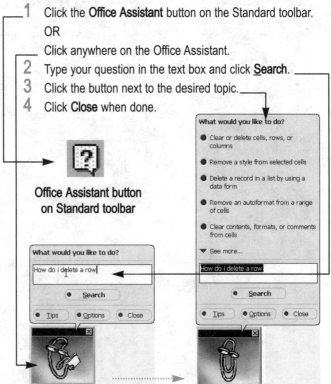

Office Assistant button on Standard toolbar

About Cells

Cells are areas in a worksheet in which you store data. You refer to cell locations by specifying their column and row positions in the worksheet. This is called a cell reference. You can enter text, values, and formulas in cells.

Notes:

- Each cell is defined by the intersection of a row and a column (e.g., A3, denoting column A, row 3). The cell's location is called a **cell reference** (or cell address).

- When you open a new workbook, it usually contains multiple worksheets. Each worksheet contains 256 columns and 65,536 rows. Therefore, each worksheet contains 17,033,216 cells!

- **Columns** are labeled A through IV, while **rows** are numbered 1 - 65,536.

- Each cell can store up to 32,000 characters.

- To select a cell, just click it, or press any arrow key in the direction of the cell you want to select. For more information about moving around in a worksheet, see *Navigate Worksheet*.

About Cell Locations

In the illustration below, cell B2 is the selected cell in Sheet1. You know this because:

- The reference B2 appears in the **name box**.

- Excel has outlined the column heading B and the row heading 2.

- Sheet1 is the highlighted tab in the workbook window.

  The contents of the selected cell appear in the formula bar.

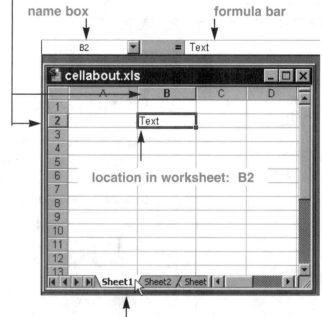

name box

formula bar

location in worksheet: B2

location in workbook: Sheet1

Cell Location in a Workbook

About Cell Properties and Controls

Cells are defined by the intersection of a column and a row. Therefore, the dimensions of a cell are defined by the column width and the row height. All cells have borders and fill properties. Selected cells have darkened borders and a fill handle (controls). These controls let you perform actions on the cell with the mouse.

Border control: You can drag the border of the selected cell to move its contents. *(See Move Cell Contents.)*

Border style: You can apply line styles to one or more of the borders of a cell. *(See Format Cell Borders and Fill.)*

Fill: You can color or shade a cell to distinguish it from other cells. *(See Format Cell Borders and Fill.)*

Fill handle: You can drag the fill handle of selected cells to extend their content as a series, or, for a single cell, to copy its content to adjacent cells. *(See Fill Cells with a Series.)*

Height/width: You can change the column width and row height to adjust the size of a cell. *(See Adjust and Hide Columns and Adjust and Hide Rows.)*

Location: You can identify the location of the selected cell by reading its cell reference in the **name box** (see illustration on previous page). You can insert cell references in formulas. For example, the formula =B2+C4 adds the values stored in those cells. *(See About References.)*

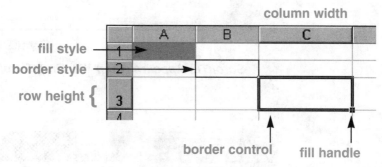

Cell Properties and Controls

Navigate Workbooks

You can use the mouse or the keyboard to move (navigate) to specific cells in a worksheet. When moving between worksheets you need to use the mouse. The new microsoft mouse provides extra navigation features.

Notes:

- **Scrolling** moves an area of data into view without changing the active cell.

- The **size of the scroll boxes** are proportional to the dimensions of the data in the current worksheet.

- Excel shows the destination row or column (**ScrollTips**) when you drag a scroll box.

Scroll to an Area in Worksheet

TO MOVE:	CLICK:
one column left or right	left or right **scroll arrow**
one row up or down	up or down **scroll arrow**
one screen up or down	vertical **scroll bar** above or below scroll box
one screen right or left	horizontal **scroll bar** to right or left of scroll box

TO MOVE:	DRAG:
to any column with data	horizontal **scroll box**
to any row containing data	vertical **scroll box**

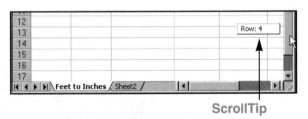

ScrollTip

ScrollTip Appears when You Drag Scroll Box

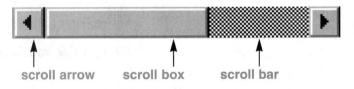

scroll arrow   scroll box   scroll bar

Horizontal Scroll Bar

Use Keyboard to Move to a Cell

Notes:

- To use a combination key like **Ctrl+Home**, press and hold the **Ctrl** key while you tap and release the **Home** key, then release **Ctrl**.

TO MOVE:	PRESS:
one cell right	**Tab**
one cell down	**Enter**
one cell left or right	**left** or **right** arrow key
one cell up or down	**up** or **down** arrow key
first cell in worksheet	**Ctrl+Home**
last cell with data in worksheet ...	**Ctrl+End**
first column in worksheet	**Home**
one screen up or down	**PgUp** or **PgDn**

Notes:

- The **sheet tabs** indicate the names of worksheets, charts, and modules in the workbook. Clicking a sheet tab displays that sheet in the workbook window. The active sheet tab is shown in bold, i.e., Feet to Inches in the illustration. You can insert, delete, move and rename sheet tabs. *(See Sheet Tabs.)*

Select a Worksheet

1 If necessary, click tab scroll arrows to bring desired sheet tab into view.

2 Click desired sheet tab.

9				FEET	I
10				4	
11					
12					
13					
14					
15					
16					
17					

Feet to Inches / Sheet2 /

tab scrolling buttons

sheet tabs

Use Mouse to Move to Any Cell in Workbook

1 If necessary, click tab scroll arrows to bring desired sheet tab into view.

2 Scroll to desired area in worksheet *(see previous page)*.

3 Click desired cell.

Select Cells, Columns, and Rows

When working with worksheets, you will need to select a cell or range of cells to complete a variety of tasks. A range may consist of adjacent or nonadjacent cells. You can also name and select named cell ranges. Keyboard shortcuts for selecting cells can be found in online Help, on the Index tab, under "keyboard shortcuts."

Notes:

- Excel will scroll the worksheet when you drag the selection beyond the visible area of the worksheet. The first cell you select becomes the active cell (cell A2 in the illustration).

Select Adjacent Cell Range

1 Click first cell you want to select.

2 Drag mouse in direction of cells to include in selection.

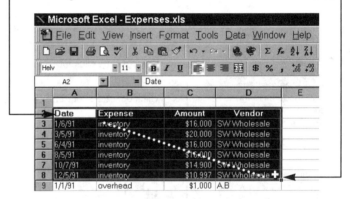

Notes:

- The first cell in the last range you select becomes the active cell (cell C2 in the illustration).

- Selecting nonadjacent cell ranges or multiple selections is often used to designate data to be included in a chart.

Select Nonadjacent Cell Range

1 Click first cell and drag in direction of cells to select.

2 Press and hold **Ctrl** while dragging through additional ranges to include in your selection.

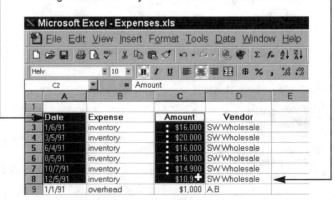

Select Entire Column or Row

- Click row or column heading to select.

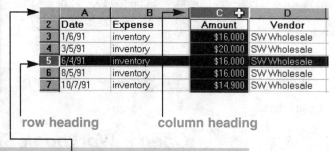

row heading   column heading

TIP: You can click the Select All button to quickly select the entire worksheet.

Name a Range

1 Select the range to name.

2 Click in the **name box** and type descriptive name.

   NOTE: Range names cannot include spaces. They may contain uppercase and lowercase letters, numbers, and most punctuation characters. The underscore character is useful for simulating a space, as in "inventory_expenses."

3 Press **Enter**.

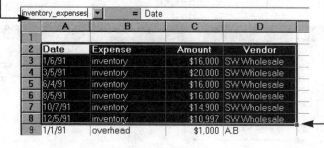

Select a Named Range

- Click in **name box**, then click name to select.

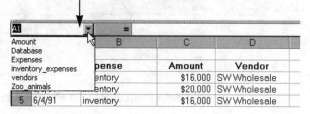

Open Workbooks

The Open command lets you open workbook files stored in previous work sessions on disk. When you click the Open button on the toolbar or select Open from the File menu, Excel presents a dialog box containing tools for displaying, finding, and opening workbook files.

Open button

🗐 File ➜ 🖙 Open...

Notes:

- In **step 2**, there are many ways to locate your workbook files. If the file you want is in the current folder, you can ignore these options and just go to step 3.

- You can change the default file location. *(See Set General Options.)* The name of the current folder (Excel) appears in the **Look in** box.

Open a Workbook Stored on Disk

1 Click the **Open** button on Standard toolbar.
2 Use any of the following methods to locate a workbook:
   - Select drive or folder containing workbook in **Look in** box.
   - Double-click a folder from the folder list to open it.
   - Select a specific folder by typing its path in the **File name** box.
   - Select parent folder of current folder by clicking the **Up One Level** button on toolbar.
   - Change view of items in document list by clicking desired button on toolbar.
3 Click desired workbook, then click **Open**.

view of items

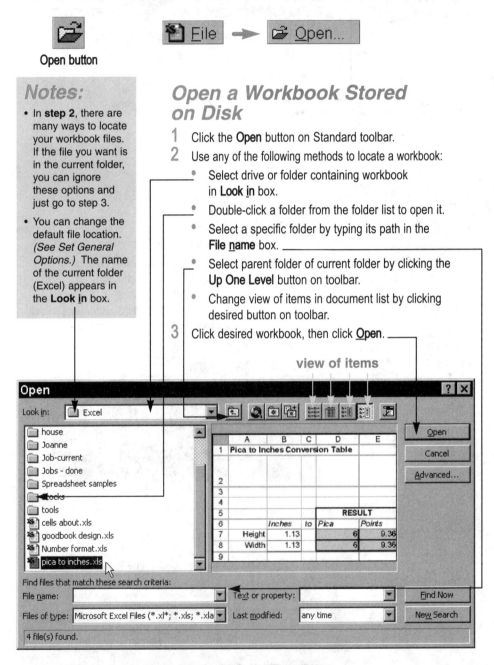

Open Dialog Box in Preview View

Use the Look in Box to Select Source Folder

1 Click the **Look in** box arrow.
2 Click desired folder name.

Sort Items in Folder/ Document List

1 Click the **Details** button on toolbar.
2 Click the column heading to sort by.

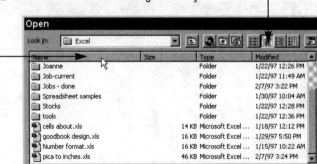

Folders and Files in Name Order

27

Save Workbooks

The Save command lets you store workbook files on disk, so you can open them in future work sessions. When you are saving a file for the first time, or saving and renaming a file (File, Save As), Excel presents a dialog box containing tools for naming the workbook and changing the destination folder.

Save button

📄 File ➡ 💾 Save / Save As...

Notes:

- The **Save As** dialog box will appear when you save a workbook for the first time, or when you use the **Save As** command.

- Use **Save As** when you want to save and rename the current file to create a new version.

Save Workbook on Disk

- Click the **Save** button on Standard toolbar, or, if saving and renaming file, click **File** menu, then **Save As**.

   If the Save As dialog box appears:

- Select drive or folder in **Save in** box.
- Double-click a folder to open it.
- Select a specific folder by typing its path in the **File name** box.
- Select parent folder of current folder by clicking the **Up One Level** button on toolbar.
- Change view of items in document list by clicking desired button on toolbar.
- Type name in **File name** box, then click **Save**.

name of current folder

view of items

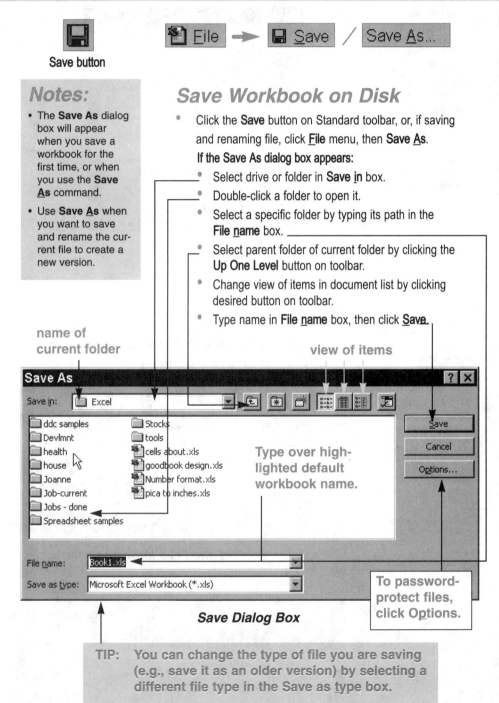

Type over highlighted default workbook name.

To password-protect files, click Options.

Save Dialog Box

TIP: You can change the type of file you are saving (e.g., save it as an older version) by selecting a different file type in the Save as type box.

28

Notes:

- The folders in the **Save in** box are displayed in a hierarchical order starting with the root folder:

  The Desktop
    My Computer
      Drive C
        My Documents
  and so on.

- You cannot drill down into subfolders from the **Save in** box list. Instead, you must select a folder, then double-click that folder's subfolder in the document/folder list.

Use the Save in Box to Change Destination Folder

1 Click the **Save in** box arrow. ———
2 Click desired folder name.

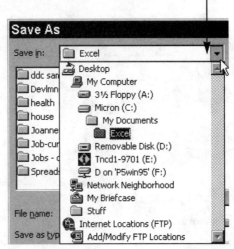

Notes:

- **More tools:** You can right-click an empty area of the folder/document list and click **Explore** to open Windows Explorer. Explorer provides a full range of file management tools.

Add a New Folder

1 Click the **Create New Folder** button on toolbar.
2 Type name for folder in **Name** box, then click **OK**. ——
3 Double-click the new folder to open it.

New Folder Dialog Box

TIP: From the file list, you can right-click a file to open a shortcut menu to perform these file tasks: Save, Quick View, Send To, Cut, Copy, Create Shortcut, Delete, Rename, Properties.

TIP: You can save your worksheet for use on the Internet: Click File menu, then click Save as HTML.

Close Workbooks and Quit Excel

When you close a workbook, Excel continues to run in computer memory. When you close (quit) Excel, all workbooks are closed, and Excel is also removed from computer memory. In either circumstance, Excel will prompt you to save open workbooks, if you have not done so already.

close button

🗐 File ➝ **Close** / **Exit**

Notes:

- In **step 1**, be sure to click the **close** button for the *workbook*, not the close button for the Excel application window.

- After **step 1**, you will be prompted to save the workbook, if changes were made to it. If not, Excel will just close the workbook.

- When prompted to save changes, you can click **Cancel** to undo the close command.

- You can close without saving changes to revert to a previously saved version of the workbook file. *(See Save Workbooks and Open Workbooks.)*

- **Other ways to close a workbook:**

  Press **Ctrl+W**.
  or
  Double-click **workbook control** icon.
  or
  Click **File** menu, then click **Close**.

Close Workbook Using Close Button

- Click **close** button on workbook window.

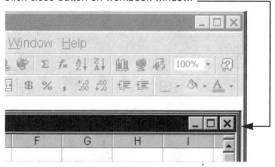

If the following dialog box appears:

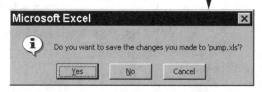

- Click **Yes** to save the changes made to the file.
  (See Save Workbooks.)
  OR
  Click **No** to close without saving.
  CAUTION: If you close without saving a workbook, you cannot undo that action.
  NOTE: When the workbook window is maximized, its window controls appear just below the Excel window as shown below.

◄— Excel
◄— workbook

Notes:

- In **step 1**, be sure to click the **close** button for the *Excel application*, not the **close** button for the workbook window.

- After **step 1**, you will be prompted to save any open workbooks, if changes were made to them. If not, Excel will just close.

- When prompted to save changes, you can click **Cancel** to undo the close command.

- **Other ways to close Excel:**

  Press **Alt+F4**.
  or
  Double-click **Excel control** icon.
  or
  Click **File** menu, then click **Exit**.
  or
  Right-click **Excel** button on Windows taskbar, then click **Close**.

Close Excel Using Close Button

- Click **close** button on Excel window.

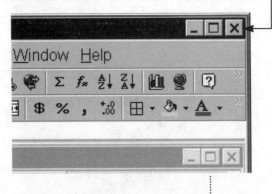

If the following dialog box appears:

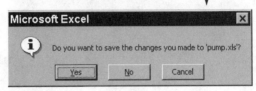

- Click <u>Yes</u> to save the changes made to the file. *(See Save Workbooks.)*

  OR

  Click <u>No</u> to close without saving.

  CAUTION: If you close without saving a workbook, you cannot undo that action.

NOTE: When Excel prompts you to save open workbooks, the prompt will look like the illustration below, if the Office Assistant is active.

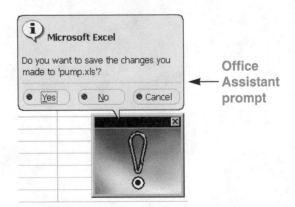

Office Assistant prompt

31

Basic Skills

This section contains illustrated procedures arranged in alphabetical order, covering a variety of basic workbook skills.

Adjust and Hide Columns

Data appears in cells defined in part by the column width. You can control the width of columns as well as hide them using the procedures in this topic. You can also adjust columns while previewing how your workbook will print *(see Print Preview)*.

Format ➡ Column

Notes:

- In **step 2**, the pointer indicates when you can perform the action. It must be a cross with left- and right-facing arrows, as shown in the illustration to the right.

- The width of the column is measured in the number of characters of the standard font.

Change Column Width Using the Mouse

1 To set width of multiple columns in one step:

Drag through column headings of columns to change.

OR

Press **Ctrl** and click column headings to change.

2 Rest pointer on right border of any selected column heading.

Pointer becomes a cross with left- and right-facing arrows.

3 Drag pointer left or right to decrease or increase the column size.

Excel displays width (in characters) in a pop-up box.

| C2 | ▼ | = | 33333 | Width: 8.57 |

	A	B	C	D
1				
2			############	
3				

column headings   cell pointer

Notes:

- In **step 1**, you can select multiple columns, but each column will adjust to the same size.

- In **step 2**, the pointer indicates when you can perform the action. It must be a cross with left- and right-facing arrows.

Automatically Size Column to Fit Largest Entry

1 Rest pointer on right border of column heading.

Pointer becomes a cross with arrows facing left and right.

2 Double-click.

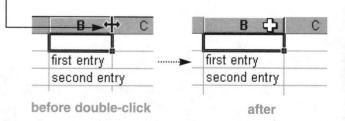

B	C
first entry	
second entry	

B	C
first entry	
second entry	

before double-click   after

Notes:

- You can hide columns to prevent others from seeing the data they contain, or just to temporarily bring columns of data next to each other for charting or other purposes.

- Prior to **step 1**, you can drag through column headings to select and hide multiple columns.

Hide Columns by Dragging

1 Rest pointer on right border of any selected column heading.

   Pointer becomes a cross with left- and right-facing arrows.

2 Drag pointer left beyond its own left border.

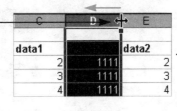 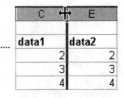

before   after

Notes:

- In **step 1**, the pointer indicates when you can perform the action. It must be a cross with double vertical line and left- and right-facing arrows.

Display Hidden Columns by Dragging

1 Rest pointer just to the right of column heading border.

   Pointer becomes a cross with a double vertical line and left and right-facing arrows.

2 Drag pointer right to display the hidden column.

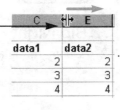

before   after

Notes:

- In **step 1**, when unhiding columns, select columns before and after hidden columns.

Adjust Columns Using the Menu

1 Select column(s) to adjust.

2 Click **Format** menu, then point to or click **Column**.

3 Click desired column command.

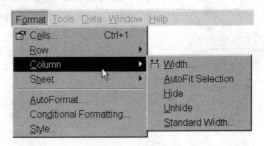

Adjust and Hide Rows

Data appears in cells defined in part by the row height. You can control the height of rows as well as hide rows using the procedures in this topic.

Format ➡ Rows

Change Row Height Using the Mouse

1 **To set width of multiple rows in one step:**

Drag through consecutive row headings of rows to change.

OR

Press **Ctrl** and click row headings to change.

2 Rest pointer on lower border of any selected row heading.

Pointer becomes a cross with up- and down-facing arrows.

3 Drag pointer up or down to increase or decrease row height.

Excel displays height (in points) in a pop-up box.

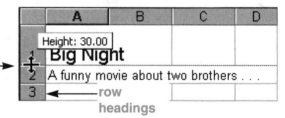

Automatically Size Row to Fit Largest Entry

1 Rest pointer on lower border of row heading.

Pointer becomes a cross with up- and down facing arrows.

2 Double-click.

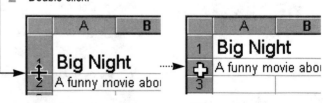

before double-click   after

Notes:

- You can hide rows to prevent others from seeing the data they contain, or just to temporarily bring columns of data next to each other for charting or other purposes.

Hide Rows by Dragging

1 To hide multiple rows, drag through row headings to hide.
2 Rest pointer on lower border of row heading to hide.
   Pointer becomes a cross with up- and down-facing arrows.
3 Drag pointer **up** beyond its own upper border.

	A	B	C
1	Date	Expenses	Amount
2	1/6/97	inventory	$16,000
3	1/7/97	inventory	$20,000
4	1/8/97	inventory	$16,000
5	Totals		$52,000

	A	B	C
1	Date	Expenses	Amount
5	Totals		$52,000
6			
7			

Notes:

- In **step 1**, the pointer indicates when you can perform the action: It must be a cross with double horizontal line and up- and down-facing arrows.

Display Hidden Rows by Dragging

1 Rest pointer just below row heading border.
   Pointer becomes a cross with a double vertical line and up- and down-facing arrows.
2 Drag pointer down to display hidden row(s).

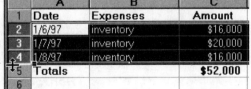

	A	B	C
1	Date	Expenses	Amount
5	Totals		$52,000
6			

	A	B	C
1	Date	Expenses	Amount
2	1/6/97	inventory	$16,000
3	1/7/97	inventory	$20,000
4	1/8/97	inventory	$16,000
5	Totals		$52,000
6			

Notes:

- In **step 1**, when unhiding rows, select rows above and below hidden rows.

Adjust Rows Using the Menu

1 Select row(s) to adjust.
2 Click **Format** menu, then point to or click **R**ow.
3 Click desired row command.

Align Data in Cells

Aligns cell data horizontally and vertically; applies text controls (wrap text in cells, shrink text to fit, merge cells); orients text in a variety of angles.

Format → ☞ Cells... ⌐ Alignment ⌐

Notes:

- If no alignment is set, Excel applies the **General alignment** which automatically left-aligns text and right-aligns values.

- If text cannot fit in a cell, you can increase the column width or select the **Shrink to fit** option *(see next page)*.

Align Cell Data Using Toolbar

1 Select cell(s) to align.

> *NOTE: To select cells that are nonadjacent, you can press **Ctrl** and click or drag through cells to include in the selection.*

2 Click desired alignment button on the Formatting toolbar:

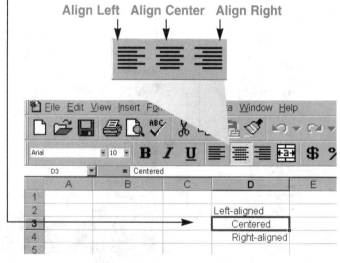

Align Left   Align Center   Align Right

Horizontal Alignment Examples

Merge and Center

1   Select cell containing data and extend selection to include cells in which data will be centered.

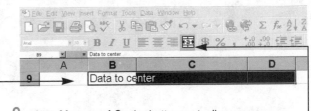

2   Click **Merge and Center** button on toolbar.

Merge and Center Example

Menu Alignment Options

You can set alignment options from a dialog box.

1   Select cells.
2   Click **Format** menu, then click **Cells**.
3   Click the **Alignment** tab.
4   Select desired options and click **OK**.

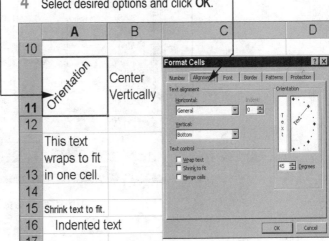

Menu Alignment Examples

AutoCalculate

AutoCalculate automatically provides the Average, Count, Count Nums, Max, Min, or Sum for a selected range. This result is for your use and cannot be transferred to the worksheet.

Notes:

- After selecting the range to be calculated, you can right-click the mouse on the AutoCalculate section of the Status Bar and select any other function from the pop-up list.
- After selecting the desired function, the answer will appear on the Status Bar as indicated in the illustration on the next page.

Change AutoCalculate Function

1 Right-click on Status bar AutoCalculate area.
   A pop-up list of functions appears.
2 Click desired function.

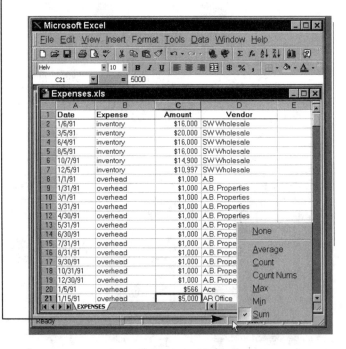

AutoCalculate Functions

40

Notes:

- AutoCalculate functions perform the following calculations on the selected range:

  None — no calculation is performed.

  Average — finds average of numbers.

  Count — counts only the numbers.

  Count Nums — counts all entries.

  Max — indicates highest value.

  Min — indicates smallest value.

  Sum — finds total of all values.

Use AutoCalculate to Find Results

1 Set desired AutoCalculate function *(previous page)*.

2 Select cells to calculate.

3 Read result that appears on the AutoCalculate area of the status bar.

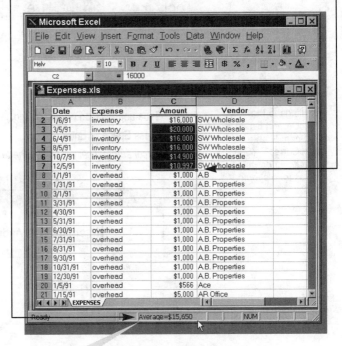

AutoCalculate Result

Average=$15,650

AutoCorrect

The AutoCorrect feature replaces misspelled words or abbreviations automatically as you type. You can change AutoCorrect options to meet your needs.

Tools → AutoCorrect...

Notes:

• You can add abbreviations and misspellings to the AutoCorrect list, or you can disable AutoCorrect. *(See remaining procedures in this topic.)*

How AutoCorrect Works

1 Select cell to receive text.
2 Type abbreviation or misspelling.
3 Press **Space** or **Enter**.
Excel automatically replaces the text.

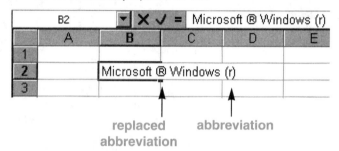

replaced abbreviation   abbreviation

Notes:

• Use this procedure to temporarily disable AutoCorrect, for example, when you don't want an abbreviation replaced. Repeat steps to enable AutoCorrect.

Disable AutoCorrect

1 Click **Tools** menu, then click **AutoCorrect**.
2 Deselect **Replace text as you type** (uncheck it).
3 Click **OK**.

deselect option

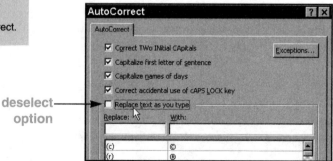

42

- It's easy to delete an abbreviation or mis-spelling from the AutoCorrect list: Just scroll to the item in the list; click the item, then click **Delete**.

- By default, AutoCorrect will:

  Correct two initial capital letters in a word.

  Capitalize first letter of a sentence.

  Capitalize names of days.

  Correct accidental use of **Caps Lock** key.

Add Abbreviations or Misspellings to AutoCorrect List

1 Click **Tools** menu, then click **AutoCorrect**.
   The AutoCorrect dialog box appears.

2 Type text to replace in **Replace** box.

3 Type replacement text in **With** box.

4 Click **Add**.

5 To add more items, repeat steps 2-4.

6 Click **OK** when done.

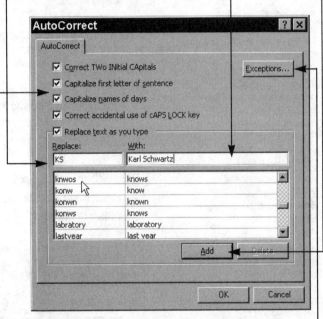

Other corrections AutoCorrect will make.

> **TIP:** Click **Exceptions** to add to Excel's list of First Letter and Initial Caps exceptions. For example, Excel might consider an unknown abbreviation as the end of a sentence. To fix this, just add the abbreviation to the "Don't capitalize after" list.

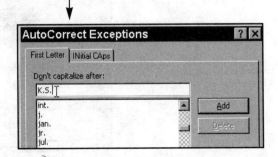

Clear Cell Contents

Clears cell contents without adjusting surrounding cells. Using menu commands, you can clear cell formats, contents, comments, or all of these items.

Edit ➡ Clear

Notes:

- In **step 1**, Excel will perform the clear command on all the cells you select in one step.

- In **step 2**, **right-click** means to press the right mouse button when the pointer is resting on any cell you have selected in step 1.

- After you clear cells, you can the click **Edit** menu, then **Undo** to reverse the operation.

- In illustration on this page, notice that after the **Clear Contents** command, the surrounding cells do not change position, and the format of the cell is retained (bold font in example).

Clear Cell Contents

Removes the contents (data and formulas) and leaves the cells blank in the worksheet, without removing formats or comments that may be applied to the cells.

1 Select cells to clear.

> NOTE: To select cells that are nonadjacent, you can press **Ctrl** and click or drag through cells to include in the selection.

2 Press **Delete**.

OR

- Right-click any selected cell.

  A shortcut menu appears.

- Click **Clear Contents**.

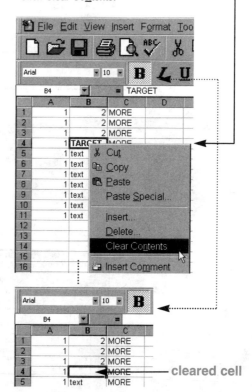

cleared cell

44

Notes:

- In **step 2**, you can point to the **Clear** command on the menu (without clicking) to open the submenu shown in the illustration on the right.

- **Comments** are notes that you can insert into a cell. Excel displays comments when you rest the pointer on a cell containing a comment. A red triangle in the upper-right corner of a cell indicates the cell contains a comment. *(See Insert, Edit, and Remove Comments.)*

Clear Cell Options Using Menu

Clears cell formats, contents, comments, or all of these items.

1 Select cells to clear.

> NOTE: To select cells that are nonadjacent, you can press **Ctrl** and click or drag through cells to include in the selection.

2 Click **Edit** menu, then **Clear**.

3 Click one of the following:

All	to clear formats, contents, and comments.
Formats	to clear only formats, such as border styles and font attributes.
Contents	to clear just the contents of the cell.
Comments	to clear just the comment attached to the cell.

Excel clears the cells as directed by your command.

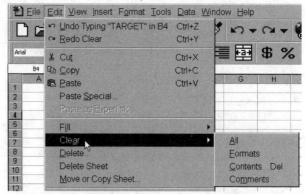

Clear Options on Edit Menu

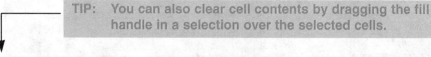

TIP: You can also clear cell contents by dragging the fill handle in a selection over the selected cells.

Pointer changes to a cross when you rest it on fill handle.

Copy and Paste Special

After copying data, you can use the Paste Special feature to apply the copied data in a variety of ways. For example, the Values option lets you copy just the result of a formula; the Add operation lets you copy the value and add it to existing data in the destination cell.

| Edit | → | 🖺 Copy | / | Paste Special... |

Notes:

- The **Paste Special** command includes a variety of paste options.

- **Paste** options copy all or an aspect of the source data or format:

  All – copies all cell contents and formatting.

  Formulas – copies only the formulas as entered.

  Values – copies only the displayed value.

  Formats – copies only the cell formats.

  Comments – copies only notes that are attached to the cells.

  Validation – copies validation rules *(see CELL DATA: Validating).*

  All except borders – copies all cell contents, except border formatting.

Copy Cell Data in Special Ways

1 Select cells to copy.
2 Click **Edit** menu, then click **Copy**.
   A flashing dashed outline appears around data.
3 Select destination cell.
4 Click **Edit** menu, then click **Paste Special**.
   The Paste Special dialog box appears.

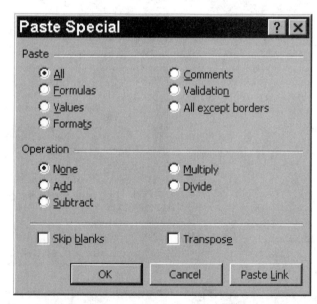

5 Select the desired options (refer to notes for details).
6 Click **OK**.
   OR
   Click **Paste Link** to establish a reference to the source data.

   *NOTE: **Paste Link** is often used to insert a reference to values stored in other workbooks.*
   Excel pastes data as specified by your selected options.

- **Operation** options, located in the **Paste Special** dialog box, let you combine source and destination data. These options are only available when **All**, **Values**, **Formulas**, or **All except borders** are selected.

  Mathematical operations include: **None**, **Add**, **Subtract**, **Multiply**, and **Divide**.

- Other Paste Special options:

  Skip blanks — tells Excel not to overwrite data in the destination cells when the source cells are blank.

  Transpose — changes the orientation of the range you are copying to a row or a column.

  Paste Link — establishes a lasting connection to the source data that will cause the destination cells to show changes made to the source cells. Paste Link is often used to link data on different workbooks or worksheets.

  The **Paste Link** command is only available when **All** or **All except Borders** is selected.

Link Data on Different Worksheets Using Paste Special

1 Select cell in sheet to copy.
2 Click **Edit** menu, then click **Copy**.

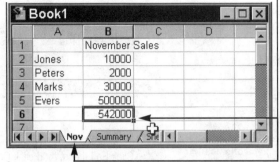

3 Select sheet, then cell in sheet to receive the link.
4 Click **Edit** menu, then click **Paste Special**.
5 Click **Paste Link**.

Excel creates linked reference to cell in source sheet.

linked reference

| B2 | ▼ | = | =Nov!$B$6 |

Book1

	A	B	C	D	
1	Yearly Sales				
2	Nov	542000			
3	Dec				
4	Jan				
5					
6					
7					

This value will change, if value in Nov sheet in cell E6 changes.

Tip: In steps 2 and 4, you can right-click the selection to access the **Copy** and **Paste Special** commands from a shortcut menu.

Copy Cell Contents

You can copy the data in one cell to other cells in a variety of ways. The method you choose often depends upon the location of the data and the destination.

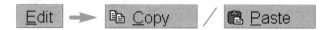

Edit → 📋 Copy / 📋 Paste

Notes:

- Using menu commands to copy cells is best when both the source and destination cells are *not* in the same viewing area.

- In **step 2**, the flashing dashed outline remains until you press **Esc**. This indicates you can repeat the paste operation.

- In **step 2** and **step 4**, you can also right-click the selection to select the **Copy** and **Paste** commands from a shortcut menu.

- **Caution:** When you paste data, existing data in the destination cells will be replaced. You can click **Edit** menu, then **Undo** to reverse the paste operation, however.

- In **step 4**, to avoid overwriting data, click **Insert** menu, then click **Copied Cells**. The Insert Paste dialog box will appear from which you can choose the direction to shift the existing cells.

Copy Cell Data Using Menu Commands

1 Select cells to copy.

2 Click **Edit** menu, then click **Copy**.
   A flashing dashed outline appears around data.

3 Select destination cell.

4 Click **Edit** menu, then click **Paste**.

5 Repeat steps 3 and 4 to repeat paste operation.

6 Press **Esc** to turn off the paste option.

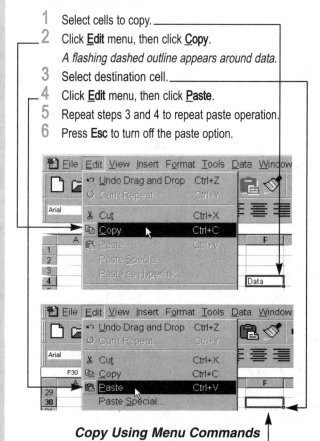

Copy Using Menu Commands

Tip: If you intend to paste the data once, you can bypass steps 4-6 and just press Enter.

48

Copy Cell Contents by Dragging Cell Border

1 Select cell(s) to copy.

2 Point to any border of selected cell(s).

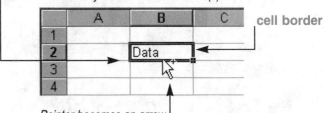

cell border

Pointer becomes an arrow.

3 Press **Ctrl** and drag border outline to new location.

4 Release mouse button.

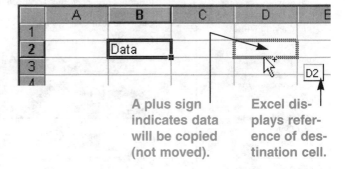

A plus sign indicates data will be copied (not moved).

Excel displays reference of destination cell.

Copy Cell Contents by Dragging Fill Handle

Crosshair appears when pointer rests on fill handle.

1 Select cell(s) to copy then point to fill handle.

A crosshair appears.

2 Drag crosshair to extend border over adjacent cells to fill.

3 Release mouse button.

Excel copies data into all cells within extended border.

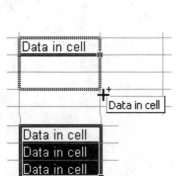

Customize Excel

The Customize command lets you customize toolbars, toolbar buttons, menu commands, and shortcut keys, so you can get your work done faster.

Tools ➞ Customize...

Notes:

• Other Toolbar options:

You can restore original settings for a toolbar by selecting it and clicking **Reset**.

You can create a new toolbar, by clicking the **New** button. *(See procedures that follow.)*

You can **Rename** and **Delete** toolbars that you create. If a built-in toolbar is selected, these options will not be available.

You can use the **Attach** command to make sure that a custom toolbar is always available with a specific workbook.

Show or Hide Toolbars

1 Click **Tools** menu, then click **Customize**.
  The Customize dialog box appears.

2 If necessary, click the **Toolbars** tab.

3 Click the name of the toolbar you want to hide or show.

4 Click **Close** when done.

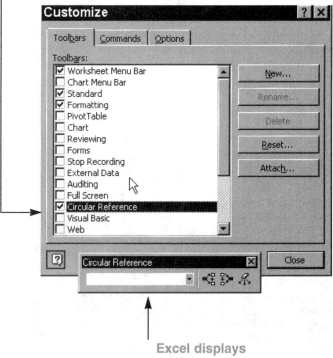

Excel displays toolbar as soon as you check the option.

Create a Custom Toolbar and Add Commands to It

1 Click **Tools** menu, then click **Customize**.

The Customize dialog box appears.

2 If necessary, click the **Toolbars** tab (see previous page).

3 Click **New**.

4 Type name for toolbar in **New Toolbar** dialog box, then click **OK**.

New floating toolbar appears.

5 Click the **Commands** tab.

6 Select the command category in the **Categories** box.

7 Drag desired commands in **Commands** list onto custom toolbar.

8 Click **Close** when done.

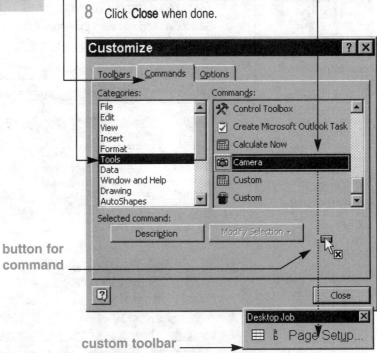

button for command

custom toolbar

TIP: In step 7, you can also drag commands onto the Excel application menu bar. When you do, Excel will open the menu and indicate where it will be inserted on the menu as you move the mouse.

TIP: The Options tab contains settings for large icons, menu animation, and ScreenTips display.

Delete Cells, Columns, or Rows

You can delete cells, entire columns, or rows from a worksheet. Existing cells adjust to take the place of the removed cells. Do not confuse Delete with Clear. Clearing cells removes only the data, while deleting cells removes the cells from the worksheet.

Edit → Delete...

Notes:

- In **step 1**, to select cells that are nonadjacent, you can press **Ctrl** and click or drag through cells to include in the selection.

- If deleted cells have been used in formulas, the formulas will display #REF! error messages. If references to adjusted cells exist in formulas, Excel adjusts the formulas, even if the reference types are absolute.

- **Caution:** You can lose data with the delete action. However, you can click **Edit** menu, then **Undo** to reverse the action.

Delete Cells Using Menu

1 Select cells to delete.
2 Click **Edit** menu, then click **Delete**.
   The Delete dialog box appears.
3 Select direction you want existing cells to shift.
4 Click **OK**.

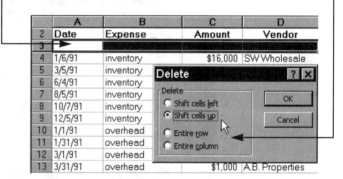

	A	B	C	D
2	Date	Expense	Amount	Vendor
3				
4	1/6/91	inventory	$16,000	SW Wholesale
5	3/5/91	inventory		
6	6/4/91	inventory		
7	8/5/91	inventory		
8	10/7/91	inventory		
9	12/5/91	inventory		
10	1/1/91	overhead		
11	1/31/91	overhead		
12	3/1/91	overhead		
13	3/31/91	overhead		$1,000	A.B. Properties

Delete

Delete
- Shift cells left
- Shift cells up
- Entire row
- Entire column

OK   Cancel

TIP: In step 2, you can also right-click any selected cell, then click Delete from the shortcut menu that appears.

	A	B	C	D
2	Date	Expense	Amount	Vendor
3				
4	1/6/91	✂ Cut	,000	SW Wholesale
5	3/5/91	▤ Copy	,000	SW Wholesale
6	6/4/91	📋 Paste	,000	SW Wholesale
7	8/5/91	Paste Special...	,000	SW Wholesale
8	10/7/91		,900	SW Wholesale
9	12/5/91		,997	SW Wholesale
10	1/1/91	Insert...	,000	A.B
11	1/31/91	Delete...	,000	A.B. Properties
12	3/1/91	Clear Contents	,000	A.B. Properties
13	3/31/91		,000	A.B. Properties
14	4/30/91		,000	A.B. Properties
15	5/31/91	🗎 Insert Comment	,000	A.B. Properties
16	6/30/91		,000	A.B. Properties
17	7/31/91	🖾 Format Cells...	,000	A.B. Properties
18	8/31/91	Pick From List	,000	A.B. Properties

Shortcut Menu

Delete Entire Column or Row

1 Click row or column heading to select.

2 Click **Edit** menu, then click **Delete**.

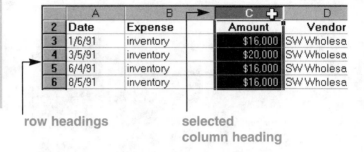

row headings

selected column heading

TIP: You can also delete cells by pressing Shift and dragging the fill handle in a selection over the selected cells.

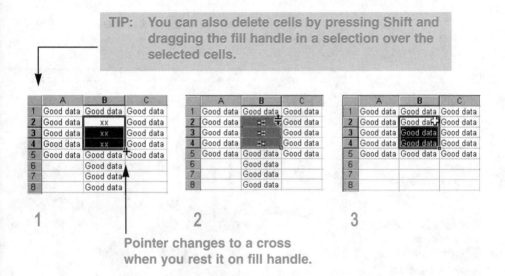

1   2   3

Pointer changes to a cross when you rest it on fill handle.

Draw Objects

This topic will introduce you to drawing objects using Microsoft Excel. Be careful: The surprising array of drawing tools may take you away from your numbers for a long while.

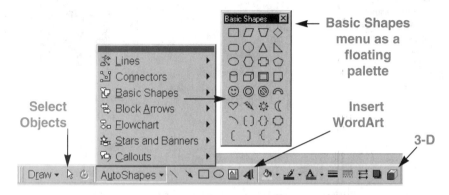

Drawing Toolbar with Open AutoShapes Menu

Notes:

- The illustration contains three graphic objects:

  WordArt — 3D Text objects.

  AutoShape — the shaded callout with text.

  Rectangle — basic AutoShape with a fill texture applied.

- Notice that the WordArt is in front of the rectangle. To change the order of any graphic object, you need only right-click the object; click **Order**, then select an option such as **Bring to Front**.

  Details about how these example objects were drawn follow on the next page.

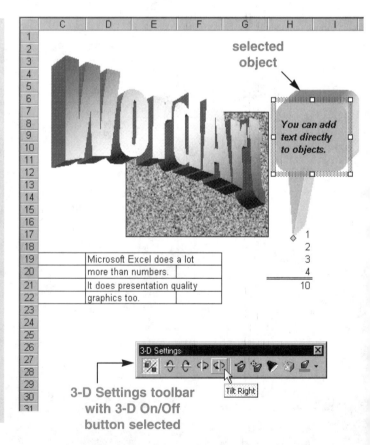

Drawing Objects and 3-D Settings Toolbar

- **WordArt**:

  Rest your pointer on each button on the WordArt toolbar to identify its purpose. Notice that you can edit the text of the selected WordArt object by clicking the **Edit Text** button.

- **3-D toolbar**:

  Rest your pointer on each button on the **3-D Settings** toolbar. With an object selected, use each of the buttons to change the object.

  If you use the **3-D Settings** toolbar on an object that is not 3-D, Excel converts it to a 3-D object.

- **AutoShapes**:

  Basic shapes, such as Line, Arrow, Rectangle, and Oval, on the Drawing toolbar are also considered AutoShapes.

  You can change the selected AutoShape object: Click the **Draw** button on Drawing toolbar; click **Change AutoShape** and select a shape from the menus that appear. Excel redraws the object, while maintaining formats you applied to it earlier.

  You can change the font format for text in an object: Drag through the text; right-click the selection, then click **Format AutoShape**.

Introduction to Drawing, by Example

- If necessary, click the **Drawing** button on the Standard toolbar to display the Drawing toolbar.

Create WordArt

1 Click the **Insert WordArt** button on Drawing toolbar.
  The WordArt Gallery dialog box appears.
2 Double-click the desired designed box.
3 Type the text: **WordArt**, then click **OK**.
  WordArt graphic appears with sizing boxes.
  WordArt toolbar also appears.
4 Drag the sizing boxes to change the object size.
5 Drag within the object to change the object position.

Open the 3-D Toolbar

1 Click the **3-D** button on Drawing toolbar.
2 Click **3-D Settings**.
3 With WordArt object selected (click it), use desired **Tilt** tools on 3-D Setting toolbar to change object angle.

Create Bubble Callout (AutoShape)

1 Click **AutoShapes** button on Drawing toolbar, point to **Callouts**, then click a bubble shaped callout in the menu.
  Pointer changes to a small crosshair.
2 Drag pointer to form the size and shape of the callout.
3 Click the **3-D** button on Drawing toolbar, then click the sample shape in upper-left corner of menu.
4 Type the text: **You can add text directly to objects.** in the box that appears in the callout object.
5 Size and position the callout object as you did the WordArt.

Create a Simple Rectangle and Fill Effect

1 Click the **Rectangle** button on Drawing toolbar.
  Pointer changes to a small crosshair.
2 Drag pointer to form the size of object.
3 Right-click the object, then click **Format AutoShape**.
4 From the **Colors and Lines** tab, click **Color** box, then click **Fill Effects**.
5 From the **Texture** tab, click desired effect, then click **OK** to close all dialog boxes.

Edit Cell Data

What you have typed in a cell can be changed (edited) with a variety of techniques. When cell editing is enabled, the formula bar displays extra controls (buttons) and displays the cell contents both in the cell and in the formula bar.

Notes:

- There are three ways you can begin to edit a cell entry:

  Double-click the cell.

  Click the cell, then click in the formula bar.

  Click the cell, then press **F2**.

- When editing:

  Excel displays a flashing cursor that indicates where new input will be inserted.

  You can press the **Ins** key to toggle between insert and overwrite mode.

  The formula bar changes to include the **Cancel**, **Enter** and **Edit Formula** buttons illustrated on the next page.

  You can insert data from the Clipboard, by pressing **Ctrl+V**.

Edit a Cell Entry by Double-Clicking

1 Double-click cell containing data to edit.

Excel displays a flashing insertion pointer in the entry and extra controls next to the formula bar.

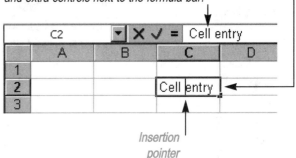

Insertion pointer

2 Click in the entry to place the insertion pointer.

OR

Drag through characters to select (next action will replace or delete your selection).

3 Edit the entry as needed:

- Type characters to insert.

- Press **Del** to delete characters to the right of insertion pointer or to delete the selection.

- Press **Backspace** to delete character to the left of the insertion pointer or to delete the selection.

4 Press **Enter**.

OR

Click ✓ on formula bar.

MOUSE HELP: To double-click, press and release left mouse button twice.

Notes:

- Replacing cell data by typing over it is best when little or none of the original cell data will be retained.

Replace a Cell Entry

1 Select cell containing data to replace.
2 Type new data.
3 Press **Enter**.
   OR
   Click ✓ on formula bar.

Notes:

- Use **Esc** to undo your changes prior to completing it.
- If you have already entered the change, you can click the **Edit** menu, then **Undo.**

Cancel Changes to a Cell Entry

Prior to entering the change:

- Press **Esc**.
  OR
  Click ✗ on formula bar.

Notes:

- By default, Excel lets you edit cell contents directly in the cell. If you need to set this option, click **Tools** menu, then **Options**; select the **Edit** tab; then select **Edit directly in cell**.

Formula Bar and Related Controls

Name box	Displays cell reference (C2) of the data you are editing.
Cancel button ✗	Lets you cancel a revision before completing it.
Enter button ✓	Lets you complete the revision with a mouse click.
Edit Formula button	Provides help when editing formulas.
Formula bar	Lets you edit the cell content.

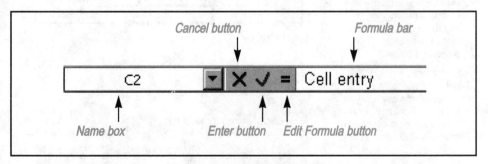

Formula Bar and Related Controls

Enter Cell Data

Entering data is very straightforward. There are, however, many techniques for entering data of different types, such as dates, times, fractions, percents, and formulas.

Enter Text or Whole Numbers

1 Select cell to receive entry.

2 Type the text or whole number.

A flashing insertion pointer appears after the data you type, and the formula bar also displays your entry.

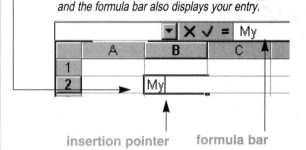

insertion pointer   formula bar

3 Press **Enter**.

OR

Click ✔ on formula bar.

Excel completes the entry and selects the cell below it.

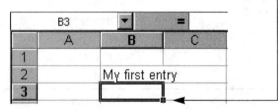

To cancel the entry before completing it:

- Press **Esc**.

OR

Click ✖ on formula bar.

Tip: To enter identical data in multiple cells, select cells, type data, then press Ctrl+Enter.

58

Enter Special Kinds of Data

1 Select cell to receive entry.

2 Type the data as shown in samples in the table below.

A flashing insertion pointer appears after the data you type, and the formula bar also displays your entry.

3 Press **Enter**.

Category:	Example of what to type:
Currency	$25,000.25
Date	6/24/97
	24-Jun
	24-Jun-97
	Jun-97
Date and time	6/24/97 10 AM
Fraction	0 1/2
Label	text
Mixed number	1 1/2
Number	25
Number as label	="25"
Percent	25%
Time	10 AM
Formula (simple)	=A1+B1

Tip: To enter today's date, press Ctrl+; (semicolon).

How AutoComplete Works

The AutoComplete feature assists you when you enter repeating text in a column.

1 Select cell to receive text.

2 Type part of the text.

Excel automatically completes the entry (see highlighted text in illustration below) based on data that it finds in the column.

Categories
vegetable
stone
vegetable

NOTE: Type over the highlighted text, if you want to change it.

3 Press **Enter**.

59

Fill Cells with a Series

The Fill Series feature extends the values in existing cells to adjacent cells that you select. This time-saving feature lets you project future values (such as trends), or extend dates or even days of the week.

Edit → Fill → Series...

Notes:

- In **step 1**, **series data** may include numbers, dates, and special lists, such as text that indicates the day of the week.

- In **step 2**, the **fill handle** is a small box in the lower-right corner of the selection. The pointer changes to a crosshair when positioned properly.

- In **step 3**, you can use the **left** mouse button. However, Excel will fill the series with the default values for your data, without giving you the option to choose.

- In **step 5**, the available fill options will depend on the kind of data you've selected.

Fill Cells with a Series by Dragging

1 Select cells containing series data.

2 Point to fill handle.

A crosshair appears.

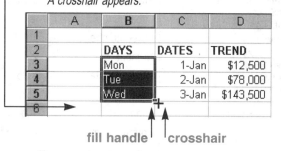

fill handle crosshair

3 Press and hold **right** mouse button and drag crosshair to extend border over adjacent cells to fill.

Excel displays default fill value in a pop-up box.

4 Release mouse button.

Excel displays fill options on shortcut menu.

5 Click fill option appropriate to your data.

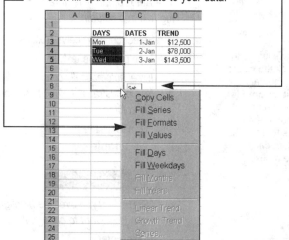

Notes:

- In **step 1**, your selection determines where the series will end, although a **Stop value** setting in step 4 can override the selection method.

- In **step 4**, you have the following options:

  Series in (Rows or Columns) lets you change the orientation of the series.

  Type lets you specify the type of calculation that will determine the series. Available options will depend on the data in your selection.

  Date unit lets you specify the kind of date units to apply.

  Trend lets you calculate future values (Linear or Growth).

  Step value lets you specify increments the series will increase by.

  Stop value lets you set the value at which the series will end, instead of using your selection.

Use Menu to Fill Cells with a Series

Use this method when you want to control exactly how the series is calculated.

1 Select cells containing existing series data and extend selection to adjacent cells you want to fill.

2 Click **Edit** menu, then point to **Fill**.

3 Click **Series** on the pop-up menu.

The Series dialog box appears.

4 Select options appropriate to your data.

5 Click **OK** when done.

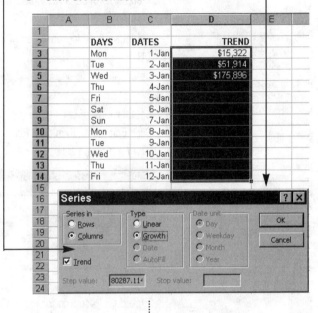

Trend Calculated By Setting in Series Dialog Box (Above)

61

Find and Replace

The Find and Replace feature can be a real time-saver. It lets you find information in one or more spreadsheets and gives you the option to replace it with new information that you specify.

Edit ➡ 🔍 Find... / Replace...

Notes:

- In **step 1**, to select multiple sheets, press **Ctrl** and click desired sheet tabs.

- In **step 2**, you can also press **Ctrl+F**.

- In **step 3**, you can search for specific formulas or data, results of calculations, and comments.

- In **step 4**, the **Look in** box provides options for where to look. For example, if you want to find the result of a formula, select **Values**. If you want to find a specific formula, select **Formulas**.

- Other Find options:

  Select the **Match case** option, when you want Excel to find only data that matches the case of your search string.

  Select the **Find entire cells only**, when the entire cell must contain your search string.

  You can change the direction that Excel searches (By Rows, or By Columns) in the **Search** box.

Find Data in Worksheets

Finds contents of cells (formulas, data), results of calculations (values), and comments.

1 Select any cell to search all of the current worksheet.

   OR

   Select sheets to search.

   OR

   Select range of cells to search.

2 Click **Edit** menu, then click **Find**.

   The Find dialog box appears.

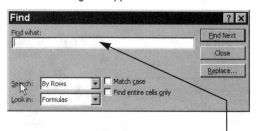

3 Type data to search for in the **Find what** box.

   NOTE: You can use the *?* (question mark) to match any single character, and you can use * (asterisk) to match any group of consecutive characters.

4 Select where the data is located in the **Look in** box.

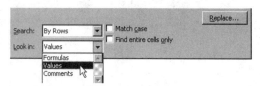

5 If required, change other options as described in the notes at the left.

6 Click **Find Next**.

   Excel selects first cell containing data you have specified.

7 Click **Find Next** again, or click **Close** when done.

- In **step 1**, to select multiple sheets, press **Ctrl** and click each sheet you want to select.

- In **step 2**, you can also press **Ctrl+H**.

- In **step 3**, you can search for specific formulas or data, results of calculations, and comments.

- In **step 5**, select the **Match case** option, when you want Excel to find only data that matches the case of your search string. Select the **Find entire cells only**, when the entire cell must contain your search string.

- **Caution:** Be careful when using the **Replace All** command, because it is easy to obtain unexpected results. For example, if you replace all instances of AND with JOIN, Excel will change words like BAND to read BJOIN. To avoid this type of error, consider using space characters in the **Find Word** and **Replacement** text boxes. That is, find spaceANDspace and replace it with spaceJOINspace.

- You can undo Replace actions: Click **Edit** menu, then **Undo**.

Replace Data in Worksheets

Finds and replaces data in worksheet, as it exists in the formula bar; does not search for comments or results of calculations.

1 Select any cell to search all of the current worksheet.

OR

Select sheets to search.

OR

Select range of cells to search.

2 Click **Edit** menu, then click **Replace**.

The Replace dialog box appears.

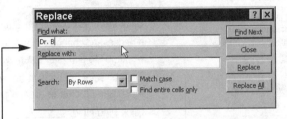

3 Type the data to find in the **Find what** box.

    NOTE: *You can use the ? (question mark) to match any single character, and you can use * (asterisk) to match any group of consecutive characters.*

4 Click in the **Replace with** box and type replacement text.

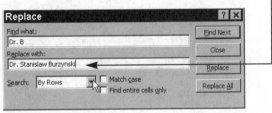

5 If desired, set options as described in the notes on the left.

6 Click **Find Next** to find the first instance.

Excel selects cell containing data.

7 Click **Find Next** to retain data in current selection and tell Excel to find the next instance.

OR

Click **Replace** to replace data in current selection.

OR

Click **Replace All** to replace data in all instances.

8 Repeat step 7 as needed, then click **Close** when done.

Find Workbooks

It can be difficult to remember just where or in what file your important work is stored. From the Open dialog box, the Find Now and Advanced (Find) commands can make this task easy to do.

Open button

🗐 File ➤ ☞ Open...

Notes:

- Find criteria options:

  File name — type all or part of file-name in this box.

  Files of type — select type of file to search for.

  Text or property — type or select text contained in the file or the file's property box. Enclose phrases in quotation marks.

  Last modified — select when the file was last changed.

Find Workbooks in Current Folder

1 Click the **Open** button on Standard toolbar.

2 If necessary, change to the folder that contains the workbook to find *(see Open Workbooks)*.

3 Type or select options in boxes in the **Find files that match these search criteria** area.

4 Click **Find Now.**

Excel displays only the files that meet your criteria.

To clear the search results and criteria:

- Click **New Search.**

5 Double-click displayed workbook to open it.

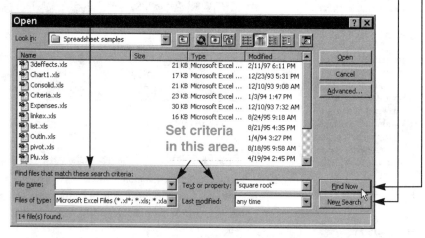

Open Dialog Box with Text or Property Criteria in Place

Notes:

- Advanced Find options:

Match case — finds only workbooks containing text that matches cases as you typed them.

Delete — removes selected criteria from list.

New Search — removes all criteria.

Save Search — lets you save the criteria for future use.

Open Search — lets you open a search criteria you saved earlier.

Find Workbook Using Advanced Find Command

1. Click the **Open** button on Standard toolbar.

   The Open dialog box appears.

2. Click **Advanced**.

   The Advanced Find dialog box appears.

   Indicate where to search:
   - Type or select starting directory in **Look in** box.
   - If desired, select **Search subfolders**.

   Add search criteria:
   - Select **And** or **Or**.
   - Select desired property in **Property** box.
   - Select desired condition in **Condition** box.
   - If available, select value in **Value** box.
   - Click **Add to List**.
   - Repeat steps to add additional criteria.

3. Click **Find Now** to begin search.

   Excel displays only folders and files containing files that meet your criteria.

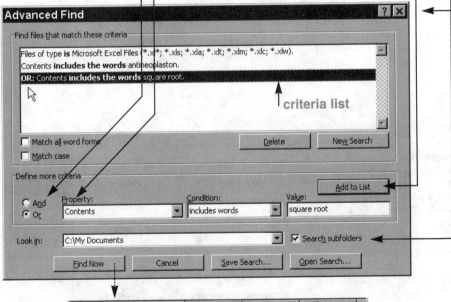

criteria list

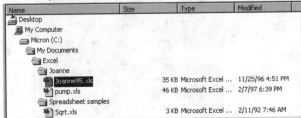

Format Cell Borders and Fill

Cells borders and fill areas can be formatted to emphasize important data in your worksheet. You can quickly apply formats using buttons on the toolbar, or you can use the Format Cells menu command to add unusual formats of your own making.

Format ➝ Cells... | Border/Patterns

Notes:

- In **step 2**, you can just click the button (not the arrow) to apply the last border used to the current cell selection.

- You can click **Edit** menu, then **Undo** to reverse the border command.

Format Borders Using Toolbar

1 Select cells to format.

2 Click the arrow on the **Borders** button on Formatting toolbar.
Excel displays a palette of common borders.

3 Click desired border.

Borders button ➝

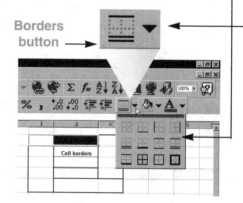

Notes:

- In **step 2**, you can just click the button (not the arrow) to apply the last fill used to the current cell selection.

- You can click **Edit** menu, then **Undo** to reverse the border command.

Format Fill Using Toolbar

1 Select cells to format.

2 Click the arrow on the **Fill Color** button on Formatting toolbar.
Excel displays a palette of common fill colors.

3 Click desired fill color.

Fill Color button ➝

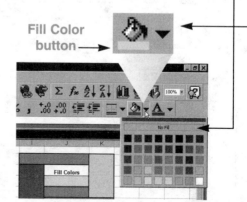

- Shortcuts to open the Format cells dialog box:

  Press **Ctrl+1**

  Right-click selection, then click **Format Cells**.

- You can quickly remove all cell borders: Select the cells, then press

  Ctrl+Shift+- (minus).

- **Border option:** You can change the color of borders by selecting a color in the **Color** box, prior to applying the border.

Format Borders and Fill Using Menu

1 Select cell(s) to format.
2 Click **Format** menu, then click **Cells**.

To apply borders:

a Click the **Border** tab.
b Click the desired line style in **Style** box.
c Click **Outline** or **Inside** button (in Presets section).

OR

Click specific location in preview area.
d Repeat steps b and c as desired.

To remove borders:

• Click the **None** button (in Presets section).

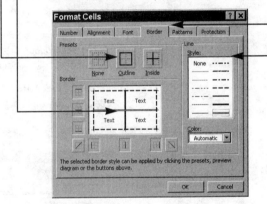

To apply fill colors:

a Click the **Patterns** tab.
b Click desired **Color**.

AND/OR

Click **Pattern** box, then select desired pattern.

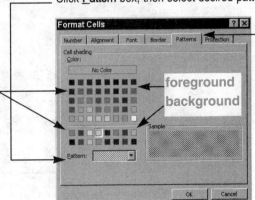

3 Click **OK** when done.

Format Cells Conditionally

This feature lets you set formats for cells and data based on their content. You can set up to three conditional formats for a given cell or range. For example, you could set up a cell to display negative values as red italic text with a cell border.

Format ➡ Con_ditional Formatting...

Notes:

- In **step 3**, the condition can refer to the contents of another cell, as in this example, or you can type a specific value (a constant), in which case you would not type an equal sign (=).

Format Cell Based on Cell Content

1 Select cell to format.
2 Click F**o**rmat menu, then click **Conditional Formatting**.
3 Set a condition in the dialog box that appears.
4 Click **F**ormat.
   The Format Cells dialog box appears.
5 Set the format for the condition and click **OK**.
6 If desired, add conditions *(see next page)*.
7 Click **OK** when done.

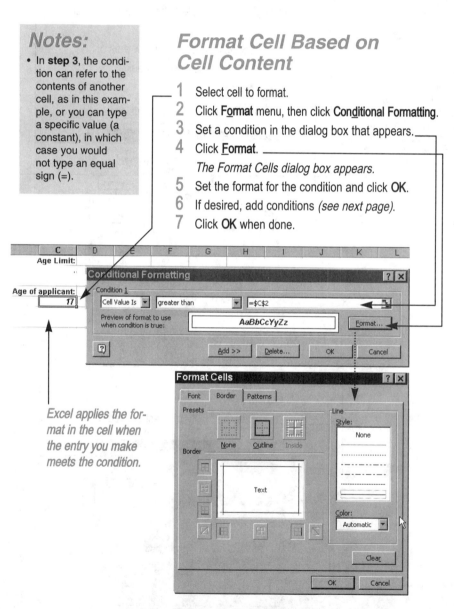

Excel applies the format in the cell when the entry you make meets the condition.

Example Using Cell Value Is Condition

68

Notes:

- You can add up to three conditional formats for a cell, and they can be **Cell Value Is** and/or **Formula Is** conditions.

- Conditional formats remain in effect until you delete them.

- You can search for cells containing conditional formats: Click **Edit** menu, then **Go To**; click **Special**, then select **Conditional Formats**).

Add and Delete Conditions

From the **Conditional Formatting** dialog box:

- Click the **Add** or **Delete** buttons..

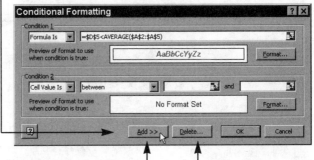

When you click Add, the dialog box expands, and you can define a second or third condition.

If you click Delete, Excel will prompt you for the condition you want to

Notes:

- The **Formulas Is** condition can evaluate cells other than the cell to which the format is applied.

- The **Formula Is** condition requires a logical formula that can be evaluated as True or False.

- You can enter a cell reference in a formula by clicking the desired cell in the worksheet.

- If a reference in a formula is located in another workbook or worksheet, you must define a name *(see Name Cells)* for the reference in the active worksheet, then use that name.

Format Cell Based on Formula

1 Follow steps in **Set Cell Format Based on Cell Content** *(see previous page)*.

2 Set the condition for **Formula Is** as shown in the example.

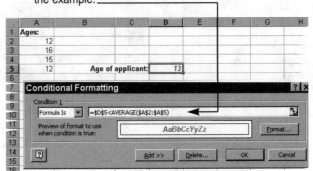

Example Using Formula Is Criteria

69

Format Cells Using Format Painter

The Format Painter button lets you copy all the formats from one cell to another in one step. It's an easy way to use the format options in the Paste Special command.

Notes:

- Format Painter copies the following formats:
  - Number
  - Alignment
  - Font
  - Border
  - Patterns
  - Protection

  Format Painter does not affect column or row height.

- After you click the **Format Painter** button, the pointer becomes a paint brush, and the source cells are outlined with dashes.

- If you make a mistake with Format Painter, you can click **Edit** menu, then **Undo** to reverse the action.

Copy Formats Using Format Painter

1 Select cells containing formats to copy.

2 Click **Format Painter** button on Standard toolbar.

3 Click on cell or drag through cell range to receive the formats.

Format Painter ➞

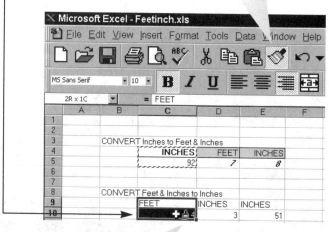

paintbrush pointer

- When you double-click the **Format Painter** button, be sure to click it again when you no longer need to copy formats.

- The source and destination cells do not have to be the same size or shape.

Copy Formats Multiple Times Using Format Painter

1 Select cells containing formats to copy.

2 Double-click **Format Painter** button on Standard toolbar.

3 Click on cell or drag through cell range to receive the formats.

Format Painter remains active.

4 Click or drag through other cell ranges as needed.

5 Click **Format Painter** button again to end process.

active
Format
Painter →

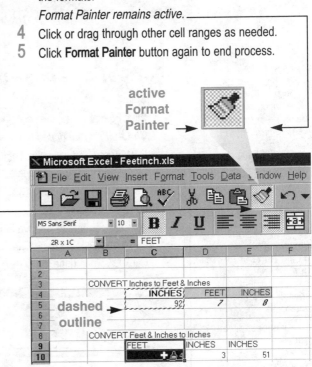

TIP: You can use Format Painter to remove all formats from cells: Just use the procedures above to copy formats of unused areas of your worksheet to the cells containing the formats you want removed.

Format Data Tables Automatically

This feature lets you quickly obtain professional-quality formats for your data. AutoFormats are combinations of formats, such as lines and fills, that Excel applies to the range of cells you indicate. All you need to do is pick the premade style you like from samples in a list.

Format → AutoFormat...

Notes:

- In **step 1**, Excel will automatically determine the surrounding cells to format. You can also select the range if you want.

- In **step 3**, consider the kind of printer you have when making your selection.

- You may want to omit a format, such as the **Number** format, when you have already applied a special format to your data.

- You cannot apply an AutoFormat if the worksheet is protected.

- You can click **Edit** menu, then **Undo** to undo the AutoFormat, if you find it unsatisfactory.

Format a Table Automatically

1   Select any cell in table.

2   Click **Format** menu, then click **AutoFormat**.
    The AutoFormat dialog box appears.

3   Click premade formats in **Table Formats** list, until you find one appropriate to your data.
    To omit specific formats:

    a   Click **Options**.

    b   Click formats to remove in **Formats to apply** area to uncheck them.

4   Click **OK** when done.

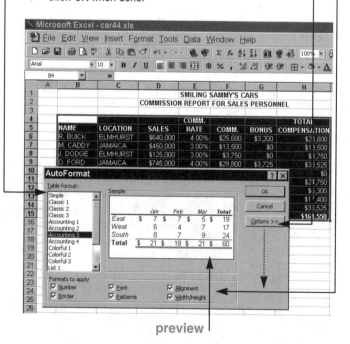

preview

AutoFormat Dialog Box

- A **PivotTable** is a special table that lets you evaluate data dynamically (*see Create PivotTables*).

- In the example below, the PivotTable changes shape when the value in the LOCATION button changes from (All) to ELMHURST. Because AutoFormat was used to format the PivotTable, the format adjusts as the table changes.

Format a PivotTable®
Automatically

For these steps refer to illustration on previous page. Sample results for a PivotTable are shown below.

1 Select any cell in PivotTable.

2 Click **Format** menu, then click **AutoFormat**.
The AutoFormat dialog box appears.

3 Click premade formats in **Table Formats** list, until you find one appropriate to your data.

To omit specific formats:

a Click **Options**.

b Click formats to remove in **Formats to apply** area to uncheck them.

4 Click **OK** when done.

	A	B	C
1	LOCATION	(All) ▼	
2			
3	Sum of SALES		
4	NAME	Total	
5	A. LEXUS	210000	
6	B. NISSAN	745000	
7	E. LINCOLN	435000	
8	J. DODGE	125000	
9	M. CADDY	450000	
10	O. FORD	745000	
11	R. BUICK	640000	
12	TOTALS	3900000	
13	V. JAGUAR	550000	
14	W. HONDA	0	
15	Grand Total	7800000	
16			

	A	B	C
1	LOCATION	(All) ▼	
2			
3	*Sum of SALES*		
4	*NAME*	*Total*	
5	*A. LEXUS*	210000	
6	*B. NISSAN*	745000	
7	*E. LINCOLN*	435000	
8	*J. DODGE*	125000	
9	*M. CADDY*	450000	
10	*O. FORD*	745000	
11	*R. BUICK*	640000	
12	*TOTALS*	3900000	
13	*V. JAGUAR*	550000	
14	*W. HONDA*	0	
15	*Grand Total*	7800000	
16			

	A	B
1	LOCATION	ELMHURST ▼
2		
3	*Sum of SALES*	
4	*NAME*	*Total*
5	*J. DODGE*	125000
6	*R. BUICK*	640000
7	*V. JAGUAR*	550000
8	*Grand Total*	1315000
9		
10		
11		
12		
13		
14		
15		
16		

How AutoFormat Adjusts as PivotTable Changes

Format Font

You can emphasize particular data by formatting the text — choosing fonts and font attributes. A font is a set of characters that share style characteristics. You can also change attributes for a given font, for example, by applying bold or italic attributes to it.

Format → 🖼 Ce_lls... ⌐ Font ⌐

Format Font Using Toolbar

1 Select cell(s) to format.

   OR

   To format only part of the text in a cell:

   a Double-click cell containing text to format.

   b Drag through text to format. ⟶ **Cell entry**

2 Select desired options on the Formatting toolbar:
   - Select desired font in **Font** box.
   - Select or type desired font size in **Font Size** box.
   - Click the **Bold** button to apply the bold attribute.
   - Click the **Italic** button to apply the italic attribute.
   - Click the **Underline** button to apply the underline attribute.

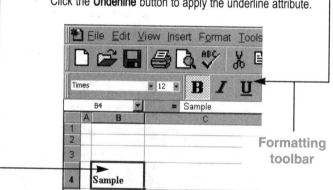

Formatting toolbar

Font box   **Font Size**   **Bold**   **Italic**   **Underline**

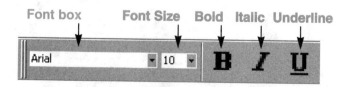

Font Controls on the Formatting Toolbar

Format Font Using Menu

- In **step 1**, you can select multiple cells by pressing **Ctrl** while you click each cell to format.

- In **step 4**, you can apply any combination of font attributes. For example, you can both bold and underline data.

- Font options:

  Select desired font in the **Font** list box.

  Select desired font style in **Font style** list box.

  Select desired font size in **Size** box.

  Select underline style in **Underline** box.

  Select font color in **Color** box.

  Select desired effect in **Effects** group.

  Click the **Normal font** check box to remove all font attributes.

- The **Preview** window shows a sample of the font and font attributes you have selected.

1 Select cell(s) to format.

OR

To format only part of the text in a cell:

a Double-click cell containing part of text to format.

b Drag through text to format. ➡ `Cell entry`

2 Click **Format** menu, then click **Cells**.

The Format Cells dialog box appears.

3 Click the **Font** tab.

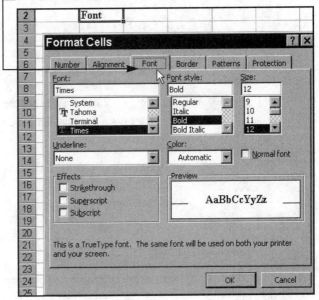

4 Select desired options as described in options in notes to the left.

5 Click **OK**.

Font	Size		
Century Gothic	14pt		
Effects			
~~Strikethrough~~	superscript	subscript	
Font styles			
Regular	*Italic*	**bold**	***Bold Italic***
Color	**Normal**	**Mixed**	
Blue	no font attributes	See Jane₂ Run ™	
Underline			
Single	Double	Single Accounting	Double Accounting

Sample Font and Font Attributes

Format Numbers

When you enter a value, Excel applies the format it thinks appropriate to your entry *(see Enter Cell Data)*. You can apply common number formats from the Formatting toolbar, such as Currency and Percentage; or you can select specific number formats using menu commands and the Format Cells dialog box.

Notes:

- When you change a number format, Excel does not change the underlying value.

- If the number cannot fit in the cell after you change the number format, Excel displays ####### (pound signs) in the cell. To fix this problem, increase the column width *(see Adjust and Hide Columns)*, or select the **Shrink to fit** option*(see Align Data in Cells)*.

- You can format a number when you enter it, by typing specific symbols, such as a $ or %.

Format Numbers Using Toolbar

1 Select cell(s) containing values to format.

   NOTE: *To select cells that are nonadjacent, you can press **Ctrl** and click or drag through cells to include in the selection.*

2 Click desired number format button on the Formatting toolbar:

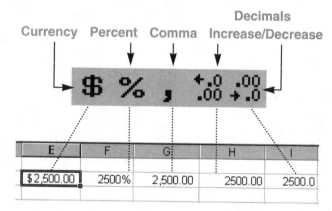

Sample Results Using Buttons on the Formatting Toolbar

- By default, Excel applies the General number format, unless you enter the number with special characters *(see Enter Cell Data)*.

- In **step 4**, the selected category indicates the current number format of the selected cell. If more than one cell is selected, and they have different number formats, no category will be selected automatically.

- The **Custom** category contains templates for all the number formats. You can select a format that is closest to the desired format, then modify it as desired. In the sample below, the custom format (date and time) shows the full year 1900.

- You can hide data in a cell by creating, then applying a custom number format. To create the format: From the **Format Cells** dialog box, select **Custom** in **Category** box, then type three semi-colons (;;;) in the **Type** box.

- Excel displays help for the selected category near the bottom of the dialog box.

Format Numbers Using Menu Commands

1 Select cell(s) containing values to format.

> *NOTE:* To select cells that are nonadjacent, you can press **Ctrl** and click or drag through cells to include in the selection.

2 Click **Format** menu, then click **Cells**.

3 Click the **Number** tab.

4 Select category of number format in **Category** list.
Excel displays options for the selected category.

5 Select options for the category you have selected.
Excel displays sample in Sample box.

6 Click **OK** when done.

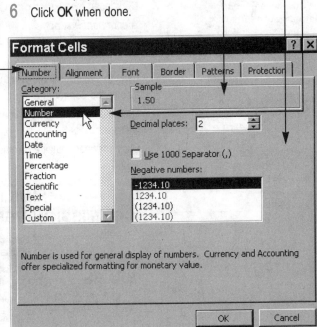

Category	Value	Comment
General	1.5	
Number	1.50	
Currency	$1.50	
Accounting	$ 1.50	
Date	January 1, 1900	*first day of century*
Time	1/1/00 12:00 PM	*first day and a half of century*
Percentage	150.00%	*you can set decimal places*
Fraction	1 1/2	
Scientific	1.50E+00	
Text	1.5	
Special	00002	*zip code*
	(718) 980-0999	*phone number*
	000-00-0002	*social security number*
Custom	1/1/1900 12:00 PM	*customized date and time*

Sample Number Formats

Insert, Edit, and Remove Comments

You can attach notes to cells by inserting a comment (formerly called cell notes). Comments do not interfere with the data in your worksheet, but they're easy to view: Just rest your mouse on the marker and the comment pops up.

Notes:

- Common uses of comments are to describe the purpose of a formula, give an operator instruction, or just to remind yourself of something that still needs to be done.

- In **step 2** you can use common editing techniques, such as selecting, formatting deleting, inserting, and pasting text.

Insert a Comment

1 Select cell to receive comment.

2 Click **Insert** menu, then click **Comments**.

   A comment box appears with your name inserted at the top.

3 Type the comment.

4 Drag the sizing handles (small squares) to change the size of the comment box.

5 Drag the border of the comment box to change its position in the worksheet.

6 Click anywhere outside comment box to close it.

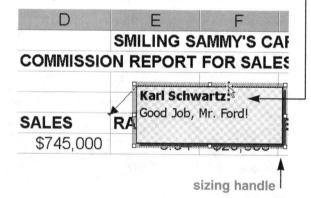

sizing handle

Notes:

- You can set Excel to always show indicator, or comment and indicator: Click **Tools** menu, then click **Options**; click the **View** tab, and select the desired Comments option.

View a Comment

- Rest pointer on comment indicator to display the comment.

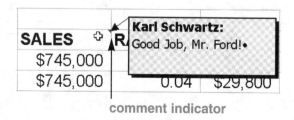

comment indicator

78

- In **step 1**, right-click means to point the cell, then click the right-mouse button once.

- With the Drawing tools on the Drawing toolbar, you can easily format the comment box.

- You can review all comments: Click the **View** menu, then click **Comments**. A **Reviewing** toolbar appears with buttons to help you navigate, edit, and create comments.

Edit a Comment

1 Right-click cell containing comment to edit.

2 Click **Edit Comment** on shortcut menu that appears.

3 Edit the comment as desired.

4 Drag the sizing handles (small squares) to change the size of the comment box.

5 Drag the border of the comment box to change its position in the worksheet.

6 Click anywhere outside comment box to close it.

LOCATION	SALES		RATE
JAMAICA	$	✂ Cut	0.04
MASPETH	$	⧉ Copy	0.04
ELMHURST	$6	📋 Paste	0.04
		Paste Special...	
ELMHURST	$5	Insert...	0.04
JAMAICA	$4	Delete...	0.03
		Clear Contents	
MASPETH	$4	Edit Comment	0.04
JAMAICA	$2	Delete Comment	0.03
		Show Comment	
ELMHURST	$1		0.03
		Format Cells...	
MASPETH		Pick From List...	0.03

Notes:

Delete a Comment

1 Right-click cell containing comment to delete.

2 Click **Delete Comment** on shortcut menu that appears.

The comment is removed, but you can undo this action, if you need to, from the Edit menu.

TIP: You can also print comments: Click File menu, then Page Setup; click the Sheet tab, then select the desired print option in the Comments box.

Insert Cells, Columns or Rows

You can insert cells, entire columns, or rows into a worksheet. Existing cells adjust to accommodate the new cells.

Notes:

- If references to adjusted cells exist in formulas, Excel adjusts the formulas, even if the reference types are absolute.

- In the illustration, inserting a cell and shifting cells down will match the salesperson with the correct location, as shown in the result below it.

- In **step 2**, you can also right-click any selected cell, then click **Insert** from the shortcut menu that appears.

Insert Cells Using Menu

1 Select cells in location where new cells will be inserted.

2 Click **Insert** menu, then click **Cells**.
   The Insert dialog box appears.

3 Select direction you want existing cells to shift.

4 Click **OK**.

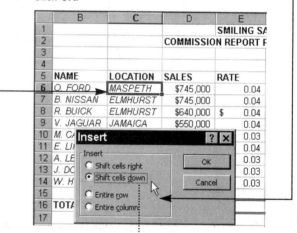

Cells Shift Down

Insert Columns or Rows Using Menu

1 Click row or column heading to select.

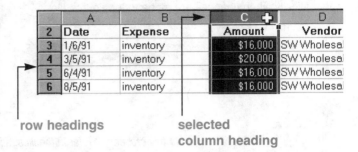

row headings   selected column heading

2 Click **Insert** menu, then click **Columns** or **Rows**.

Insert Cells, Columns, or Rows Using Shortcut Menu

1 Select cells or click or drag through row or column headings.

NOTE: The number of headings you select tells Excel how many columns or rows to insert.

2 Right-click the selection.

3 Click **Insert** on shortcut menu that appears.

	A	B	C	D
1	Date	Expense	Amount	Vendor
2	1/6/91	inventory	$16,000	SW Wholesale
3	3/5/91	inventory	$20,000	SW Wholesale
4	6/4/91	inventory	$16,000	SW Wholesale
5	8/5/91	inventory	$16,000	SW Wholesale
6	10/7/91	inventory	$14,900	SW Wholesale
7	12/5/91	inventory	$10,997	SW Wholesale
8	1/1/91	overhead	$1,000	A.B
9	1/31/91	overhead	$1,000	A.B. Properties
10	✂ Cut		$1,000	A.B. Properties
11	▤ Copy		$1,000	A.B. Properties
12			$1,000	A.B. Properties
13	▤ Paste		$1,000	A.B. Properties
14	Paste Special...		$1,000	A.B. Properties
15			$1,000	A.B. Properties
16	Insert		$1,000	A.B. Properties
17	Delete		$1,000	A.B. Properties
18			$1,000	A.B. Properties
19	Clear Contents		$1,000	A.B. Properties
20			$566	Ace
21	▤ Format Cells...		$5,000	AR Office
22	Row Height...		$5,000	AR Office
23			$5,000	AR Office
24	Hide		$5,000	AR Office
25	Unhide		$5,000	AR Office
26	6/14/91	overhead	$5,000	AR Office

Insert OLE Objects

The Insert Object command lets you insert OLE objects — collections of information, such as a Word document, into Excel. When activated, objects provide access to the tools of the application that created the file. If you insert a linked object, Excel updates it automatically when changes are made to the source file.

Insert ➜ Object...

Insert a New OLE Object

For this procedure, refer to the illustrations on the next page.

1 Select cell where you want to insert the object.

2 Click **Insert** menu, then click **Object**.
   The Object dialog box appears.

3 Select object type in **Object type** list.

4 Click **OK**.
   The object is inserted, and menus and tools for the application it belongs to appear in place of the Excel tools.

   - Use the application tools to create the document.
   - Drag the sizing handles (small squares) to change the size and shape of the object.
   - Drag the border of the object to change its position.
   - Click outside the object to return to normal editing.

To activate (edit) the object information:

   - Double-click the object.
     The source application tools replace Excel's tools.

To select and work on object as a picture:

(Also see Insert Picture — Format Picture)

   - Click the object once to select it.
     Sizing handles appear around the object.
   - To delete the selected object, press the **Delete** key.
   - To show the Picture toolbar for the object, right-click object, then click **Show Picture Toolbar**.
   - To format the selected object, right-click in its borders, then click **Format Picture.**
     OR
     Use the buttons on the **Picture** toolbar that appears when the object is inserted. Rest the pointer on each button to determine its purpose.

82

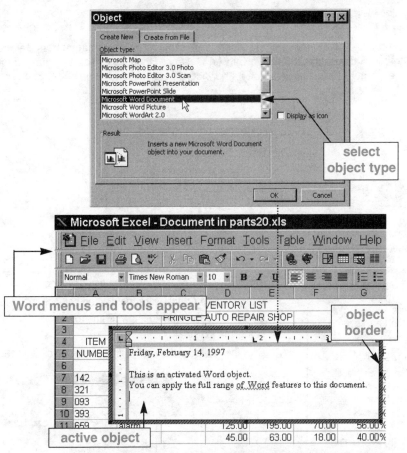

Object __Activated__ in Excel Worksheet

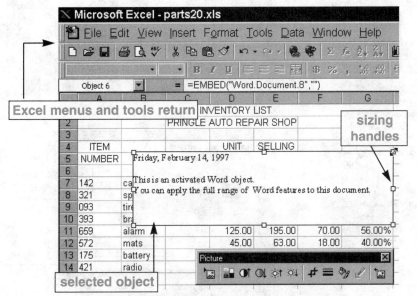

Object __Selected__ in Excel Worksheet

Insert Pictures

The Insert Picture command lets you insert sophisticated graphic images from a variety of sources, including Microsoft's own Clip Art Gallery. Once you insert a picture, Excel provides an array of tools to enhance it and incorporate it in your worksheet or chart data.

Insert → Picture

Notes:

- In **step 2**, the **Picture** submenu also contains other sources for pictures. For example, use the **From File** option to insert a graphic file you created in another application.

- Other Microsoft Gallery options:

  You can click the **Internet Explorer** button to import images stored on the internet.

  The **Clip Properties** command lets you view and change image properties.

  You can use the Help button on the title bar to examine the purposes of controls and other tabs.

- The lock and key picture in the example was modified so that the worksheet can be seen through it. To do this, right-click the image, then click **Format Picture**; click the **Colors and Lines** tab, then set **Fill Color** to No Fill and **Line Color** to No Line.

Insert Clip Art in a Worksheet

1 Click **Insert** menu, then point to or click **Picture**.
   A submenu appears.

2 Click **Clip Art**.
   The Microsoft Clip Gallery dialog box appears.

3 From the **Clip Art** tab, click the desired category of images, or click **All Categories** to show all images in the image list.

4 Click the desired picture in the image list, then click **Insert**.

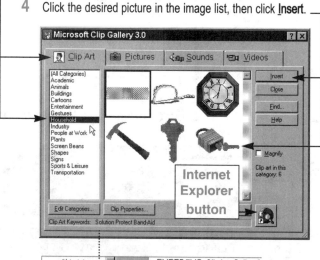

Internet Explorer button

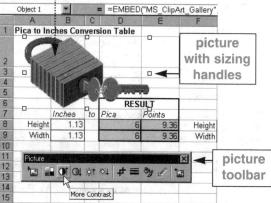

picture with sizing handles

picture toolbar

84

- In **first step**, by default, Excel displays the Picture toolbar when you select a picture.
- To hide or show the **Picture toolbar**: Right-click the picture, then click **Show Picture Toolbar**, or click **Hide Picture Toolbar**.

Format Picture

- Click image to select it.

  Sizing handles appear on the picture and the Picture toolbar will appear.

To change the size of the picture:

- Drag sizing handles in direction to size picture.

To change the position of the picture:

- Point to interior of picture and drag in the direction to move the picture.

To use Picture toolbar:

Point to any button on **Picture** toolbar to identify its purpose. Your options include:

- Change the line style of picture border
- Crop the picture
- Insert a new picture from file
- Increase or decrease brightness
- Increase or decrease contrast
- Open the Format Picture dialog box
- Reset the picture
- Set a transparent color

You can click the Format Picture button on the Picture toolbar to format the picture further.

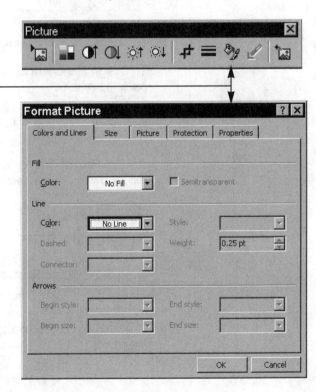

Macros

A macro is a shortcut to a series of commands that are carried out automatically when you run it. You can create macros by recording complex tasks that you repeat often. Then run the macro to execute the task quickly. This topic will show you how to record and play back (run) simple macros.

Notes:

- In **step 4**, the first character in the macro name must be a letter. Remaining characters may be numbers, letters, or the underscore character. Spaces are not valid.

- In **step 5**, if you store the macro in the **Personal Macro Workbook**, the macro will always be available for use.

- In **step 7**, if you select this option, Excel will play back the macro relative to active cell, instead of playing it back in the same cells in which it was recorded. You can turn this feature on and off to achieve different results in the same macro.

Record a Macro

1 Plan the actions you want to record.

2 Click **Tools** menu, then point to or click **Macro**.

3 Click **Record New Macro** on the submenu that appears.
The Record Macro dialog box appears.

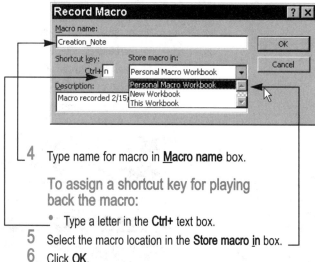

4 Type name for macro in **Macro name** box.

To assign a shortcut key for playing back the macro:

- Type a letter in the **Ctrl+** text box.

5 Select the macro location in the **Store macro in** box.

6 Click **OK**.
The Stop Recording toolbar appears indicating that you can begin recording the macro.

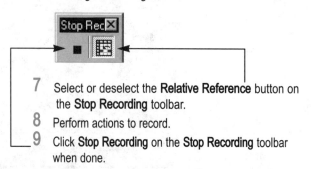

7 Select or deselect the **Relative Reference** button on the **Stop Recording** toolbar.

8 Perform actions to record.

9 Click **Stop Recording** on the **Stop Recording** toolbar when done.

Notes:

- If you need to select a graphic object without activating the macro assigned to it, first click the **Select Objects** tool on the Drawing toolbar.

Assign Macro to Graphic Object

After you assign a macro to a graphic object, you can run it by clicking the graphic.

1 Right-click graphic object.

2 Click **Assign Macro** on the shortcut menu that appears.

   The Assign Macro dialog box appears.

3 Select name of macro to assign to graphic in **Macro Name** list.

4 Click **OK**.

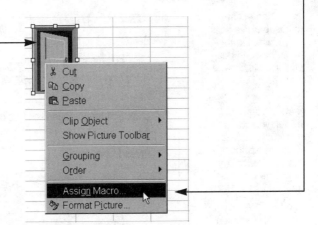

Notes:

- If a macro does not work as expected, and you want to delete it: Follow the **Using menu** steps below, then click **Delete** instead of **Run**.

- To edit a macro, you will have to learn to use the **Visual Basic Editor** and macro language. Recording macros, then examining the code, is one way to learn Visual Basic code.

Run (Play Back) a Macro

- If necessary, select cell in which macro will begin its work.

Using assigned shortcut key:

- Press key combination assigned when you created the macro, such as **Ctrl+M**.

Using assigned graphic object or picture:

- Click picture or graphic to which the macro has been assigned (see above).

Using menu:

a Click **Tools** menu, then point to or click **Macro**.

b Click **Macros** on the submenu that appears.

   The Macro dialog box appears.

c Select name of macro to run in **Macro Name** list.

d Click **Run**.

Move Cell Contents

You can move the data in one cell to other cells in a variety of ways. The best method to choose depends upon the location of the source data and its destination.

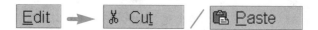

Edit → ✂ Cut / 📋 Paste

Notes:

- Using menu commands to move cells is best when both the source and destination cells are *not* in the same viewing area.

- In **step 2** and **step 4**, you can also right-click the selection to select the **Cut** and **Paste** commands from a shortcut menu.

- **Caution:** When you paste data, existing data in the destination cells will be replaced. You can click **Edit** menu, then **Undo** to reverse the paste operation.

- In **step 4**, to avoid overwriting data, you can click **Insert** menu, then **Cut Cells**. The **Insert Paste** dialog box will appear, from which you can choose the direction to shift the existing cells.

Move Cell Contents Using Menu Commands

1 Select cells to move.

2 Click **Edit** menu, then click **Cut**.
   A flashing dashed outline appears around selected cell.

3 Select destination cell.

4 Click **Edit** menu, then click **Paste**.
   OR
   Press **Enter**.

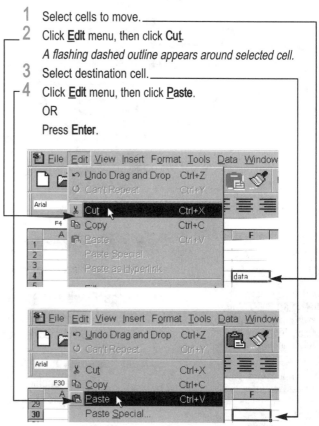

Move Using Menu Commands

88

Notes:

- The drag border method is best when the source and destination cells are nearby.

- In **step 3**, "drag" means to press and hold the left mouse button while moving the mouse.

- In **step 3**, to avoid overwriting data in destination cells, press **Ctrl+Shift** while dragging cell border. Existing cells will shift to accommodate new data.

Move Cell Contents by Dragging Cell Border

1 Select cell(s) containing data to move.

2 Point to any border of selected cell(s).

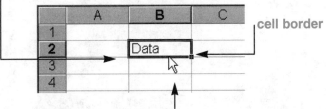

cell border

Pointer becomes a solid arrow.

3 Drag border outline to new location.

4 Release mouse button.

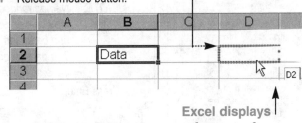

Excel displays reference of destination cell.

Notes:

- You can also use menu commands (**Edit**, **Cut** and **Edit**, **Paste**) to move a cell's content.

- If you make a mistake, you can click the **Edit** menu, then click **Undo**. Excel lets you undo multiple actions, not just your last.

Move Part of a Cell's Contents into Another Cell

1 Double-click cell containing data to move.

A flashing insertion pointer appears.

2 Drag through data to select it. ⟶

3 Press **Ctrl+X** (Cut).

4 Double-click destination cell and click where data will be inserted.

OR

5 Select cell to be overwritten by data.

6 Press **Ctrl+V** (Paste).

Excel highlights data in cell.

Name Cells

When you name a range of cells, you can quickly use the name (instead of a difficult to remember cell reference) to calculate values in the range. For example, you can create a formula, such as =sum(Salary), when Salary is a range of cells containing salary values.

Insert ➡ Name

Notes:

- Using the name box is the quickest way to create a name for a reference.

- In **step 2**, when you first click in the name box, Excel selects the active cell reference. Just type over that selection to create the name.

Name Cells Using Name Box

1 Select the range to name.

2 Click in the **name box** and type descriptive name.

> NOTE: *Named ranges cannot include spaces. They may contain uppercase and lowercase letters, numbers, and most punctuation characters. The underscore character is useful for simulating a space, as in inventory_expenses.*

3 Press **Enter**.

Inv_amount		=	16000	

	A	B	C	Ve
1				
2		name box		
3	Date	Expense	Amount	Ve
4	1/6/91	inventory	$16,000	SW Whole
5	3/5/91	inventory	$20,000	SW Whole
6	6/4/91	inventory	$16,000	SW Whole
7	8/5/91	inventory	$16,000	SW Whole
8	10/7/91	inventory	$14,900	SW Whole
9	12/5/91	inventory	$10,997	SW Whole
10	1/1/91	overhead	$1,000	A.B

Notes:

- You must first convert titles that are numbers to text. Excel converts date values to text automatically. Spaces in titles are replaced with underscore characters in the reference name.

- After creating names, click arrow in Name box to select/view names.

Name Cells Using Titles

1 Select range containing data and column or row titles.

2 Click **Insert**, menu, then point to or click **Name**.

3 Click **Create** on the submenu that appears.

4 Select location of titles in **Create Names** dialog box.

5 Click **OK**.

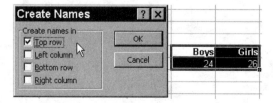

Create Names	? X
Create names in	
☑ Top row	OK
☐ Left column	
☐ Bottom row	Cancel
☐ Right column	

Boys	Girls
24	26

90

- From the **Define Name** dialog box you can also add and delete names, values, and formulas.

- **Add names:**
  Type the name in the **Names in workbook** box; define the range in the **Refers to** box, then click **Add**.

- **Delete names:**
  Click the name, then click **Delete**.

  Name formulas or values:
  Type the name in the **Names in workbook** box; define the formula or type a value in the **Refers to** box, then click **Add**.

- **Examples:**

  You might name formula =Sum(C4:C9) as Total_for_Inv. Then you could build another formula in a cell that refers to the result of that calculation.

  You might name the value 5280 as Mile. You can then build a formula in a cell that refers to that value as in =3*Mile.

Change Name Definition Using Menu

1 Click **Insert**, menu, then point to or click **Name**.

2 Click **Define** on the submenu that appears.

The Define Name dialog box appears.

3 Click the name of the reference you wish to change.

4 Click in the **Refers to** box.

Excel marks range in worksheet with a dashed line.

5 Drag through cells in worksheet to change the reference.

Excel collapses the dialog box so you can see more of the worksheet.

6 Release the mouse.

Excel expands dialog box and corrects reference.

7 Click **OK** when done.

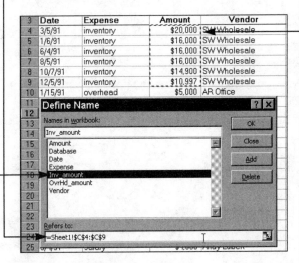

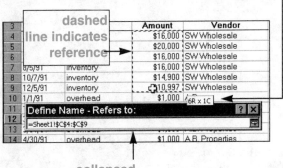

dashed line indicates reference

collapsed dialog box

Protect Workbooks

The Protect Workbook feature prevents changes to the structure of the workbook, so that its sheets cannot be moved, copied, hidden, renamed, or deleted. It also lets you prevent workbook windows from being moved or sized. You can also set a password when saving a file to restrict the workbook.

Tools ➔ Protection ➔ Protect Workbook...

Notes:

- Before protecting the workbook, check the current workbook structure and/or window arrangement to ensure it is as you like it.

- **Caution:** If you protect the workbook with a password and forget the password, you will not be able to change the workbook structure at a later time.

- The workbook protection password is case sensitive.

Protect Workbook Structure and Windows

1 Click **Tools** menu, then point to or click **Protection**.
2 Click **Protect Workbook** on the submenu that appears.
   The Protect Workbook dialog box appears.

To protect the workbook structure:
- Click the **Structure** check box to select it.

To prevent windows from being moved or sized:
- Click **Windows** check box to select it.

To protect workbook with a password:
- Type password in **Password** box.

3 Click **OK**.

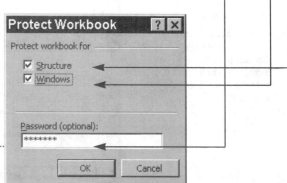

The Confirm Password dialog box appears, if you protect the workbook with a password.
Read the caution!

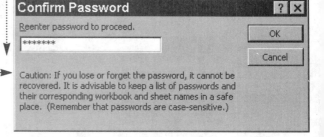

92

Notes:

- To save time, you may not want to assign a password when protecting the workbook while developing and creating it.

- The workbook protection password is case sensitive.

Unprotect a Protected Workbook

1 Click **Tools** menu, then point to or click **Protection**.

2 Click **Unprotect Workbook** on the submenu that appears.

   If you assigned a password, the Unprotect Workbook dialog box appears:

   • Type password, then click **OK**.

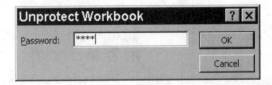

Notes:

- Save options:

  Always create backup — creates a backup of previous version of the workbook each time you save it.

  Password to open — prevents users from opening workbook without a password.

  Password to modify — prevents users from opening, changing, or saving the workbook without a password.

  Read-only recommended — sets workbook to display a read-only recommendation when opened.

- **Caution:** All passwords are case sensitive, and you will not be able to open workbooks without supplying the correct password.

Save and Protect Workbook

1 Click the **Save** button on Standard toolbar.

   OR

   If you have saved and named the file previously:

   • Click **File** menu, then click **Save As**.

   The Save As dialog box appears.

2 Click **Options**.

   The Options dialog box appears.

3 Select workbook protection options in File Sharing section of dialog box.

4 Click **OK** when done.

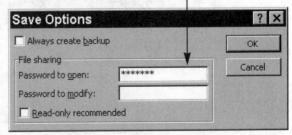

5 Click **Save** in the **Save As** dialog box.

Protect Worksheet Data

The Protect Worksheet feature lets you protect or lock an entire worksheet, individual cells, or a range of cells from accidental or unauthorized use. You can assign a password to a protected worksheet, so others cannot unprotect it without supplying the password.

Format → 🖹 Cells... ⌐ Protection ⌐

Notes:

- By default, all cells in a worksheet are locked. However, this state is activated only when the worksheet is protected (see below).

- In **step 1**, if the worksheet is protected, first unprotect the worksheet *(next page)*.

- In **step 4**, a grey check in the check box indicates that some of the cells are currently locked, while others are not.

Lock and Unlock Cells in a Worksheet

1 Select cells to unlock or lock.

2 Click **Format** menu, then click **Cells**.

3 Click the **Protection** tab. ⎯⎯⎯

4 Click **Locked** check box to select or deselect it.

To hide formulas for selected cells:

- Click **Hidden** check box to select it. ⎯⎯⎯

   NOTE: *Selecting this option prevents Excel from displaying any formulas contained in the selected cells on the formula bar.*

5 Click **OK**.

6 To enable your settings, protect the worksheet.

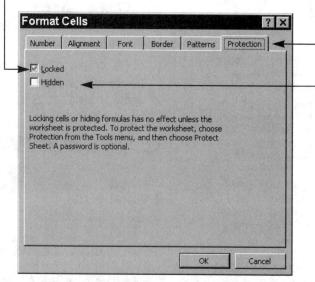

Protection Options for Cells

Notes:

- Before protecting worksheet, be sure to lock or unlock the cells you want to protect. Also, size and position objects if you plan to protect them.

- **Caution:** If you protect a worksheet with a password and lose the password, you will not be able to unprotect it.

Protect a Worksheet

1 Click **Tools** menu, then point to or click **Protection**.

2 Click **Protect Sheet** on the submenu that appears.
   The Protect Sheet dialog box appears.

3 Click the desired protection options to select or deselect them.

   Contents . . . . . . protects data in locked cells.

   Objects . . . . protects pictures, shapes, and charts.

   Scenarios . . . . . protects scenario definitions.

   To protect sheet with a password:

   a Type password in **Password** box, then click **OK**.

   b When prompted, re-enter password, then click **OK**.

4 Click **OK**.

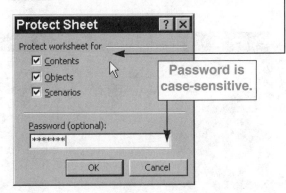

Password is case-sensitive.

Notes:

- In **step 2**, if you type the password incorrectly, you must redo steps 1 and 2, then retype the password correctly.
  Remember, passwords are case sensitive.

Unprotect Worksheet

1 Click **Tools** menu, then point to or click **Protection**.

2 Click **Unprotect Sheet** on the submenu that appears.
   If you assigned a password:

   • Type password in **Password** box when prompted.

Set Calculation Options

The Options dialog box collects related settings together in tabs. The Calculation tab lets you tell Excel how to perform calculations in your worksheet.

Tools ➡ Options...   Calculation

Notes:

• In **step 2**, you will not have to select **Calculation** tab, if it was selected the last time you opened the **Options** dialog box.

Set Calculation Options

1 Click **Tools** menu, then click **Options**.
  The Options dialog box appears.
2 Click the **Calculation** tab.
3 Select options described on the next page.
4 Click **OK** when done.

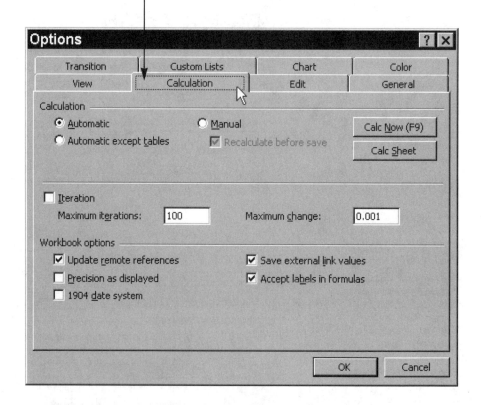

Options Dialog Box with Calculation Tab Selected

96

A̱utomatic: Automatically calculates formulas when changes are made in worksheet. This is the default calculation setting.

Automatic except ṯables: Automatically calculates formulas, but not data tables, when changes are made in worksheet. When this setting is enabled, you will have to click **Calc N̲ow** or press **F9** to calculate formulas in data tables.

M̱anual: Turns off automatic calculations. When this setting is enabled, you will have to click **Calc N̲ow** or press **F9** to calculate formulas in your worksheets. Excel automatically selects **Recalc̲ulate before save** when you select **M̲anual**.

Recalc̲ulate before save: If **M̱anual** is selected, deselect this option to disable calculations before saving the workbook.

Calc N̲ow (F9): Calculates all open workbooks and the data tables and charts they contains.

Calc S̲heet: Calculates only the active worksheet and the data tables and charts linked to it.

I̱teration: Limits the number of iterations Excel performs when goal seeking or resolving circular references (formulas that contain references to their own results).

Maximum iṯerations: Type the maximum number of iterations to perform before the iteration stops.

Maximum c̲hange: Type the maximum change that can result from the iteration before the iteration stops.

Update r̲emote references: Automatically calculates formulas containing references to other workbooks or applications.

Precision as displayed: Changes the precision stored values in cells to number format displayed in cells.

1904 d̲ate system: Changes the January 1, 1900 starting date, from which all dates are calculated, to January 2, 1904 (Macintosh date system).

Save external l̲ink values: Automatically saves copies of values from external documents to which the workbook has links. Clear this setting to reduce the time it takes to load workbooks containing links to other workbooks.

Accept labels in formulas: Enables use of label names in formulas for ranges of values that contain titles.

Set Edit Options

The Options dialog box collects related settings together in tabs. The Edit tab lets you set up the editing environment, such as direct editing in cells, and applies the settings to all worksheets in the workbook.

Tools → Options...   Edit

Notes:

• In **step 2**, you will not have to select **Edit** tab, if it was selected the last time you opened the **Options** dialog box.

Set Edit Options

1 Click **Tools** menu, then click **Options**.
   The Options dialog box appears.
2 Click the **Edit** tab.
3 Select options described on the next page.
4 Click **OK** when done.

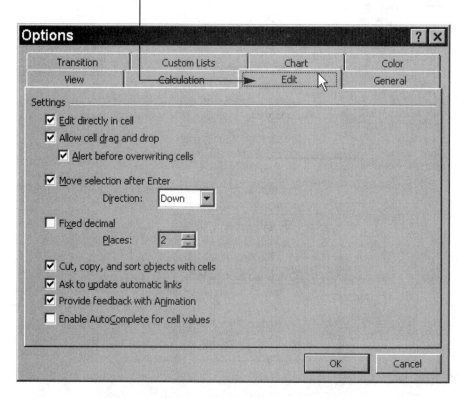

Options Dialog Box with Edit Tab Selected

- The default Edit options will work well in most instances. If your system does not have a lot of memory and is slow, however, consider disabling the **Provide feedback with Animation** option, to improve performance.

- The **Fixed decimal Places** option can save you a great deal of time. For example, if you need to enter many decimal values like .05, .55, 3.12, select **Fixed decimal** and set **Places** to 2. Then, in your worksheet, you need only type 05, 55, 312, and Excel will change the values you typed by moving the decimal left, two places, when you press **Enter**.

Edit Options

Edit directly in cell: Lets you edit cell entries in the cells, by double-clicking them. If deselected, you can edit by the same method, but you must work with the entries in the formula bar.

Allow cell drag and drop: Allows moving and copying cell contents by dragging the cell border. This option also allows you to copy data into adjacent cells, or to create a series by dragging cell's fill handle.

Alert before overwriting cells: Alerts you when existing data will be replaced when you are using drag-and-drop editing.

Move selection after Enter: Select the direction of the next active cell after you complete an entry .

Direction: Select the direction in which Excel will move to activate the next cell after each entry is completed.

Fixed decimal: Moves the decimal place to the left or right automatically. This setting changes the values you enter in cells. To override this setting, type the decimal point when you enter a number.

Places: Type the number of places to move the decimal point in your entries. Positive numbers decrease the value you type, moving the decimal two places to the left.

Cut, copy, and sort objects with cells: Keeps objects with cells when you cut, copy, filter, or sort cells.

Ask to update automatic links: Type the maximum change that can result from the iteration before the iteration stops.

Provide feedback with Animation: Animates worksheet changes, such as inserted cells or columns.

Enable AutoComplete for cell values: Enables the AutoComplete feature that completes your entries, based on existing entries in a column.

Set General Options

The Options dialog box collects related settings together in tabs. The General tab lets you set a variety of working defaults, such as the number of recently used files to display on the File menu.

Tools ➡ Options... ⌐ General ⌐

Notes:

- In **step 2**, you will not have to select **General** tab, if it was selected the last time you opened the **Options** dialog box.

Set General Options

1 Click **Tools** menu, then click **Options**.
  The Options dialog box appears.
2 Click the **General** tab.
3 Select options described on the next page.
4 Click **OK** when done.

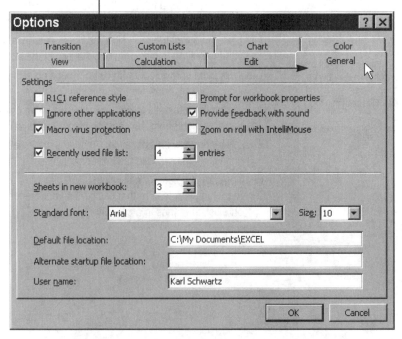

Options Dialog Box with General Tab Selected

- The default General options will work well in most instances. If you find that you are consistently adding worksheets, consider changing the **Sheets in new workbook** option.

- You may want to disable the **Macro virus protection**, if you consistently work with workbooks that contain macros and rarely work with files from unknown sources.

- The **Default file location** is worth changing, if you consistently need to change the current folder when opening or saving files.

General Options

R1C1: Changes reference style of row and column headings from letter-numbers to number-numbers, and designates references in formulas as relative to the current cell position.

Ignore other applications: Prevents the exchange of data with other applications using the DDE protocol.

Macro virus protection: Enables protection from workbooks that may contain destructive macros (viruses). When enabled, Excel will prompt you when a workbook contains macros. You can then decide to disable the macros when you open the workbook, or open the workbook with the macros enabled if you trust the source of the document.

Recently used file list: Lists recently used files at the bottom of the File menu, so you can select from the list to open a file quickly.

    entries — select number of recently opened files to list.

Prompt for workbook properties: Sets Excel to prompt for workbook properties (such as title, keywords, author) each time you save a new workbook file.

Provide feedback with sound: Plays sounds associated with Office 97 events.

Zoom on roll with IntelliMouse: Enables use of Microsoft's new IntelliMouse.

Sheets in new workbook: Type number of blank worksheets to include in new workbooks.

Standard font: Select desired default font to use for new worksheets. You must restart Excel for this change to take effect.

    Size: Select size of default font.

Default file location: Type directory path to indicate the default location of files you save or open. You must restart Excel for this change take effect.

Alternate startup file location: Type directory path to indicate location of workbooks or other files you want Excel to open automatically when you first run Excel. Files in this folder will open in addition to files stored in the XLstart folder, a folder created when you install Excel.

User name: Type your name here. One use of the user name is to identify the user of a shared workbook.

Set View Options

The Options dialog box collects related settings together in tabs. The View tab lets you set a variety of working defaults, such as whether or not to show gridlines, row and column headings, and zero values.

Tools → Options...   View

Notes:

- In **step 2**, you will not have to click the **View** tab, if it was selected the last time you opened the **Options** dialog box.

Set View Options

1 Click **Tools** menu, then click **Options**.
   The Options dialog box appears.
2 Click the **View** tab.
3 Select options described on the next page.
4 Click **OK** when done.

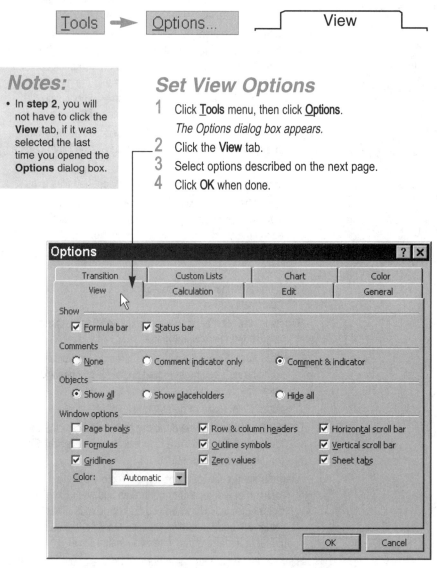

Options Dialog Box with View Tab Selected

- The **Hide all** option will even hide comments if you have enabled the **Comment & Indicator** option.

- You can deselect **Zero value** to hide the results of formulas that result in zero.

View Options

Formula bar: Displays formula bar at the top of the worksheet.

Status bar: Displays status bar at the bottom of the Excel window.

None: Hides comments and comment indicators in cells containing comments.

Comment indicator only: Shows only the comment indicator in cells containing comments. The comment itself will appear only when you rest the pointer on the indicator.

Comment & indicator: Shows both the comment and comment indicator in cells containing comments.

Show all: Shows all graphic objects and embedded charts in worksheet.

Show placeholders: Shows only placeholders for graphic objects and embedded charts in worksheets.

Hide all: Hides all graphic objects and embedded charts in worksheet.

Page breaks: Displays automatic page breaks.

Formulas: Displays formulas in cells, instead of formula results.

Gridlines: Displays cell gridlines. This setting does not affect print gridlines which are set in the Sheet tab of the Page Setup dialog box.

Color: Select a color for worksheet gridlines.

Row & column headers: Shows row and column headings.

Outline symbols: Shows outline symbols when outline mode is on.

Zero values: Shows zeros when cells contain them.

Horizontal scroll bar: Shows this scrollbar.

Vertical scroll bar: Shows this scrollbar.

Sheet tabs: Shows sheet tabs which allow you to select worksheets with the mouse.

Share Workbooks

The Share Workbooks feature lets more than one user simultaneously contribute data, revisions, and formatting to the same workbook over a network.

Tools ➞ Share Workbook...

Notes:

- When you complete the steps to enable workbook sharing, Excel will notify you that it needs to save the workbook.

- You can repeat these steps to view current users of the shared workbook. To set advanced options refer to the procedure on the next page.

- To remove a user, select the user name in the list, then click **Remove User**. The user will not be able to save the workbook, and their unsaved changes will be lost.

Enable Workbook Sharing

1 Open or create workbook to share.

2 Click **Tools** menu, then click **Share Workbook**.

The Share Workbook dialog box appears.

3 Click the check box to allow changes by more than one user, then click **OK**.

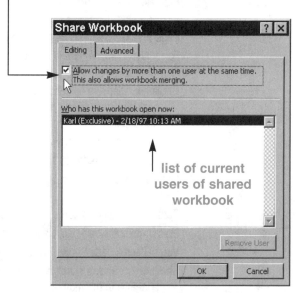

list of current users of shared workbook

Excel indicates workbook is shared.

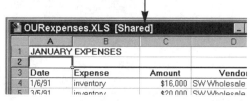

- Sharing tracks the history of changes made to the workbook by all users. It also maintains information about how users resolved conflicts when entering data in a shared workbook.

- When you save a shared workbook, Excel inserts comments in cells where data has been changed by other users.

Set Advanced Share Options

1 Open or create workbook to share.

2 Click <u>T</u>ools menu, then click S<u>h</u>are Workbook.
The Share Workbook dialog box appears.
Click the **Advanced** tab.

3 Select options described in **Advanced** dialog box, then click **OK**.

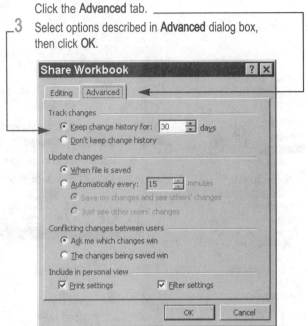

TIP: You can use the Track Changes command (<u>T</u>ools, Track Changes), to highlight or list changes (tracking history) on a new sheet.

You can then use the filter arrows to zero in on special change events. For example, you can list just the changes made by specific users.

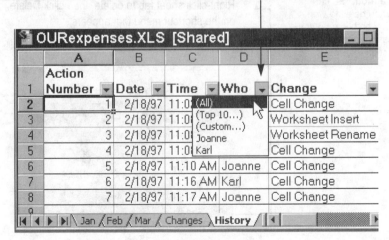

Sheet Tabs

Sheet tabs let you organize and work with multiple worksheets within a single workbook file. You can select, group, insert, rename, delete, move, and copy sheet tabs. Also see *Working with Worksheets* and *Sheet Tabs* for information about scrolling and selecting sheet tabs.

Notes:

- In **step 2**, you can also press **Shift** and click to select consecutive sheets.

  Grouped sheets appear highlighted (white), while ungrouped sheets appear grey. When sheets are grouped, The word "[Group]" appears after the workbook name on the title bar.

- You can also ungroup sheets by clicking any sheet tab that is not currently grouped.

Group and Ungroup Sheet Tabs

When you group sheets, data and formatting changes made to the active sheet are repeated in the grouped sheets.

1 Click first sheet tab in group.

2 Press **Ctrl** and click each sheet tab to add to group.

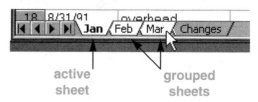

active
sheet

grouped
sheets

3 Click any grouped sheet tab to make it active.

To ungroup sheet tabs:

- Right-click any grouped sheet, then click **Ungroup Sheets** on the shortcut menu that appears.

Notes:

- **Caution:** Be careful when deleting worksheets, because you cannot undo this action.

Delete Sheet Tabs

1 Right-click sheet tab to delete, then click **Delete** on the shortcut menu that appears.

2 Click **OK** to confirm the action.

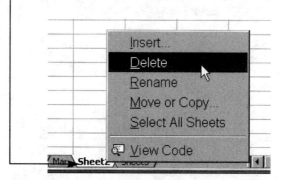

Insert a New Sheet

1 Right-click any sheet tab, then click **Insert** on the shortcut menu that appears.

   The Insert dialog box appears.

2 Click **Worksheet** icon, then click **OK**.

3 Rename and move sheet tab as desired.

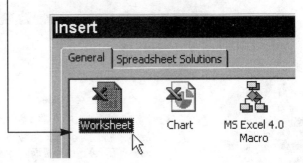

Rename a Sheet

1 Double-click sheet tab to rename.

   Excel highlights the sheet tab name.

2 Type new name, then click anywhere in worksheet.

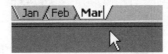

Move and Copy Sheets

1 Select sheet(s) to move or copy.

   Excel highlights the the sheet tab names.

2 To move sheets, drag selection to desired location.

triangle marks insertion point

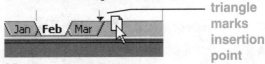

OR

To copy sheets, press **Ctrl** and drag selection to desired location.

plus sign indicates copy

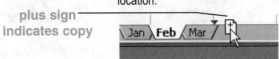

Spell Check

The Spell Check feature lets you find and correct misspelled words in your worksheets and charts. If words you use often are not in Excel's main dictionary, you can add them as they are found by the Spell Check operation. See *AutoCorrect* for information about this feature and how it corrects spelling errors as you type.

Tools ➡ ✓ Spelling...

Notes:

- In **step 1**, if you are checking a worksheet, select cell A1, to check the entire worksheet in the first pass.
  You can select multiple sheet tabs *(see Sheet Tabs)* to spell check multiple sheets in one pass.

- The **Ignore All** command tells Excel to ignore all such words found.

- The **Change All** command tells Excel to change all such words to the word in the **Change to** box.

- Once you add a word to the custom dictionary, Excel uses the main and custom dictionaries to spell check words.

Spell Check

1 Select cells or worksheets to spell check.

2 Click **Tools** menu, then click **Spelling**.

The Spelling dialog box appears when the first word not found in Excel's main dictionary is found.

The **Suggestions** box lists Excel's suggested replacements, and the first word is placed in the **Change to** box.

To leave word unchanged:

- Click **Ignore** or click **Ignore All**.

To change the word not found:

- If necessary, click desired word in **Suggestions** list.
- Click **Change** or **Change All**.

To leave word unchanged, and add it to custom dictionary:

- Click **Add**.

To leave word unchanged and add it to the AutoCorrect list:

- Click **AutoCorrect**.

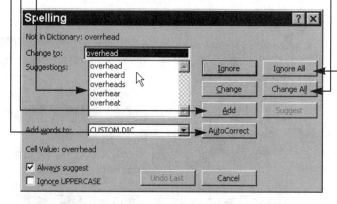

3 Click **OK** when notified that spell check is complete.

Notes:

- Sometimes when Excel finds a misspelled word, you will realize that a completely different word would be more appropriate. In a case like this, type the word you want in the **Change to** box. If you are not sure of the spelling of the word, click **Suggest**.

Look Up Words While Spell Checking

1 Select cells or worksheets to spell check.

2 Click **Tools** menu, then click **Spelling**.

The Spelling dialog box appears when the first word not found in Excel's main dictionary is found.

The **Suggestions** box lists Excel's suggested replacements, and the first word is placed in the **Change to** box.

3 Type word to lookup in **Change to** box.

4 Click **Suggest**.

Excel displays possible spellings for typed word in Suggestions list.

type word, then click Suggest

Excel displays suggestions here

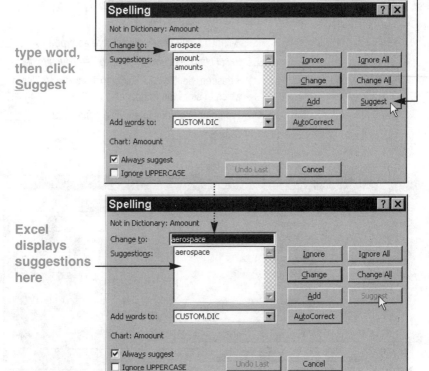

TIP: You can type any replacement text you want in the Change to box and click **Change**.

Templates

Each time you create or insert a new workbook, you are opening a very plain template. You can create custom templates for special purposes — templates containing special headings, formatting, and page setups, so that you do not have to create from scratch work that you repeat often.

Eile ➡ Save As... ➡ Save as type: Template (*.xlt)

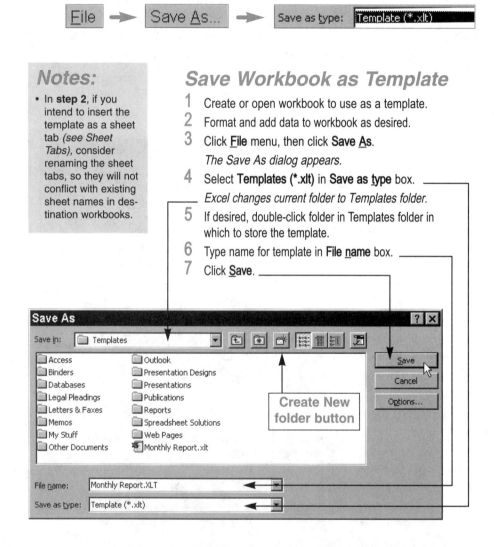

Notes:

• In **step 2**, if you intend to insert the template as a sheet tab *(see Sheet Tabs)*, consider renaming the sheet tabs, so they will not conflict with existing sheet names in destination workbooks.

Save Workbook as Template

1 Create or open workbook to use as a template.
2 Format and add data to workbook as desired.
3 Click **File** menu, then click **Save As**.
   The Save As dialog appears.
4 Select **Templates (*.xlt)** in **Save as type** box.
   Excel changes current folder to Templates folder.
5 If desired, double-click folder in Templates folder in which to store the template.
6 Type name for template in **File name** box.
7 Click **Save**.

Save As

Save in: ☐ Templates

☐ Access
☐ Binders
☐ Databases
☐ Legal Pleadings
☐ Letters & Faxes
☐ Memos
☐ My Stuff
☐ Other Documents

☐ Outlook
☐ Presentation Designs
☐ Presentations
☐ Publications
☐ Reports
☐ Spreadsheet Solutions
☐ Web Pages
☐ Monthly Report.xlt

Create New folder button

Save
Cancel
Options...

File name: Monthly Report.XLT
Save as type: Template (*.xlt)

TIP: You can create a folder by clicking the Create New Folder button on the Save As toolbar, then double-click that folder to store the file in it. The new folder name will appear as a tab in the New dialog box, when you create a new file.

110

Notes:

- By default, Excel stores templates in the **Program Files\MsOffice97\ Templates** folder. This folder can be hard to find. Therefore, when you reach this folder, consider adding it to your list of favorites by clicking the **Add to Favorites** button on the **Open** dialog box toolbar.

Edit Template File

1 Click **File** menu, then click **Open**.
2 Select **Templates (*.xlt)** in **Files of type** box.
3 Change to folder containing the template.
4 Click the file, then click **Open**.

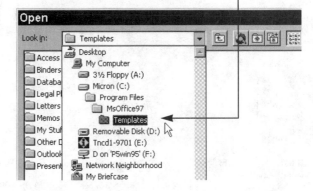

Notes:

- The **New** dialog box also appears when you insert a work-sheet tab *(see Sheet Tabs)*.

Create New File Based on Custom Template

1 Click **File** menu, then click **New**.

   The New dialog box appears.

2 If you created a folder for the template, click the tab for the folder name.
3 Click the name of the template, then click **OK**.

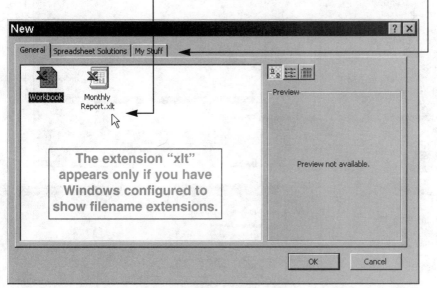

The extension "xlt" appears only if you have Windows configured to show filename extensions.

Troubleshooting

Excel contains so many features and settings that it's inevitable that you will run into trouble from time to time. However, you can turn to the Help feature, an extensive and thorough resource, for help troubleshooting your problem.

Notes:

- Microsoft Help Troubleshooting topics include:

  Active X controls
  change highlighting
  change history
  charts
  converting files
  data consolidation
  data validation
  dates
  electronic mail
  entering data
  files
  formatting cells
  forms
  formulas
  graphics
  hyperlinks
  macros
  merging workbooks
  Microsoft Excel
    customization
  number formatting
    in charts
  numbers
  Office Assistant
  opening files
  outlines
  PivotTables
  printing
  protection
  queries
  scenarios
  shared workbooks
  Solver
  spell checking
  templates
  what-if analysis

Use Help to Troubleshoot Problems

1 Click **Help** menu, then click **Contents and Index**.

2 Click the **Index** tab

3 Type **troubleshooting** in first text box.
  Excel scrolls to the item as you type the characters.

4 Click desired subtopic, then click **Display**.

5 If additional subtopics are displayed, double-click the desired subtopic.

6 Use buttons and Help window toolbar to navigate topics.

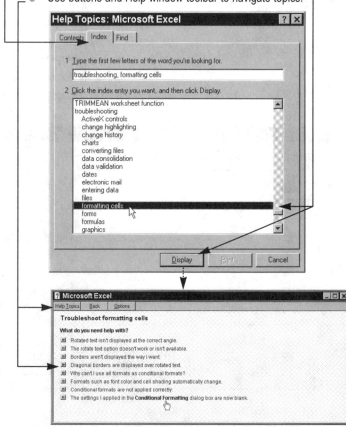

Common Causes of Displayed Error Messages

Below is a list of error values that may appear in a cell when Excel cannot calculate a formula value.

#DIV/0! — Indicates that the formula is trying to divide by zero.

Possible causes in formula: • Divisor is a zero. • Divisor is referencing a blank cell or a cell that contains a zero value.

#N/A — Indicates that no value is available.

Possible causes in formula: • An invalid argument may have been used with a LOOKUP function. • A reference in an array formula does not match range in which results are displayed. • A required argument has been omitted from a function.

#NAME? — Indicates that Excel does not recognize the name used in a formula.

Possible causes in formula: • A named reference has been deleted or has not been defined. • A function or named reference has been misspelled. • Text has been entered without required quotation marks. • A colon has been omitted in a range reference.

#NULL! — Indicates that the intersection of two range references does not exist.

Possible cause in formula: • Two range references (separated with a space operator) have been used to represent a nonexistent intersection of the two ranges.

#NUM! — Indicates a number error.

Possible causes in formula: • An incorrect value has been used in a function. • Arguments result in a number too small or large to represent.

#REF! — Indicates reference to an invalid cell.

Possible cause in formula: • Arguments refer to cells that have been deleted or overwritten with nonnumeric data. The argument is replaced with #REF!.

#VALUE! — Indicates the invalid use of an operator or argument.

Possible cause in formula: • An invalid value, or a referenced value, has been used with a formula or function, i.e., SUM("John").

Circular — A message on status bar that indicates formula is referring to itself.

Possible cause in formula: • A cell reference refers to the cell containing the formula result. The Circular Reference toolbar may appear when a circular reference is detected. You can use the toolbar to locate the circular reference and to trace the references in the formula.

NOTE: *If a circular reference is intended, you can select* **Options** *from the* **Tools** *menu, then select* **Iteration** *from the* **Calculation** *tab. Iteration is an instruction to repeat a calculation until a specific result value is met.*

113

Workbook File Properties

Workbook file properties can help you to identify and find a file. These properties automatically include statistics about the file size and when it was created and changed last. In addition, you can fill in standard fields, such as Subject and Author. To assist further in future searches for the file, you can select the "Save preview picture" option.

File → Properties

Notes:

- You will utilize the information listed in the Workbook file **Properties** dialog box when searching for a file in the **Open** dialog box.

Set Workbook File Properties

1 Click **File** menu, then click **Properties**.
   The Properties dialog box appears.

2 From the **Summary** tab, type information you want saved with the file in the field boxes provided.

To save preview of workbook:

- Click **Save preview picture** to select it.

3 Click the following tabs to display file information:

General   file type, location, size, attributes, dates.
Statistics file modification information, including user names.
Contents worksheet names.

4 To set custom properties, see next page.
5 Click **OK** when done.

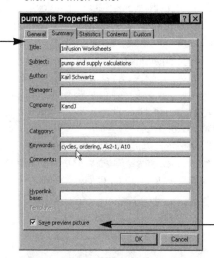

Tip: To automatically open the Properties dialog box when you save workbook for the first time, click Tools menu, then click Options. From the General tab, select Prompt for workbook properties.

114

Create a Custom Property Linked to Data in Workbook

1 Name the cells in the worksheet to which you want the link created.

2 Click **File** menu, then click **Properties**.
The Properties dialog box appears.

3 Click the **Custom** tab.

4 Type property name in **Name** box or select ready-made names in list.

5 Select type of property in **Type** list.

6 Click **Link to content** to select it.

7 Select named range in **Source** box, then click **Add**.
Excel adds custom property to Properties list.

8 Click **OK** when done.

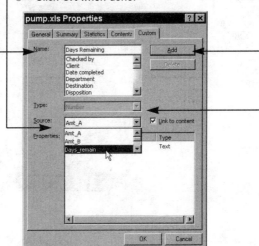

View Properties from the Open Dialog Box

1 Follow steps to open a new file *(see Open Workbooks)*.

2 Click **Commands and Settings** button on Open toolbar.

3 Click **Properties** on menu that appears.
The Properties dialog box appears.

4 Click desired tab in **Properties** dialog box.

5 Click **OK** when done.

Workbook Window Commands

You can open many workbooks simultaneously. You may want to arrange the open workbooks to see them all at one time. You may want to hide one or more workbooks, while still keeping the information they contain accessible to formulas.

Window ➡ Arrange , New Window , Hide / Unhide

Notes:

• In the illustration there are two MARKET35 workbooks. Refer to the next procedure for information about creating a new window for an open workbook.

Select a Workbook Window

• Click **Window** menu, then click name of workbook.
  Excel brings selected workbook to the front.

				H	I
	Data	Window	Help		
		New Window		100%	
		Arrange...			
		Hide			
		Unhide...			
CRAV					
TRAN		Split			
DATE		Freeze Panes		VIDEND	GAIN OR
SOLD				ARNED	LOSS
11.	✓	1 market35.xls:1			
6/3		2 market35.xls:2		585.50	-319.31
4/2		3 car44.xls		325.40	2459.71
				0.00	671.97
12/5/96	3954.69	5391.23		0.00	-1436.54
12/20/96	15487.54	14326.54		1054.50	2215.5

Notes:

• The **New Window** command lets you maintain different views for a single workbook. You can use this feature to view two worksheets in the same workbook, side-by-side.

Open New Window for Current Workbook

• Click **Window** menu, then click **New Window**.
  Excel brings selected workbook to the front and adds a number to the end of its name in title bar.

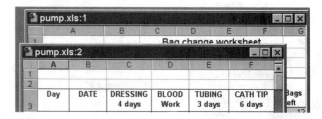

116

Arrange Workbook Windows

1 Click **Window** menu, then click **Arrange**.

   The Arrange Windows dialog box appears.

2 Select desired option, then click **OK**.

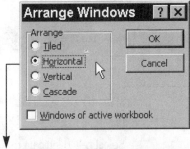

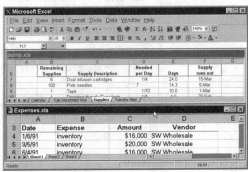

Horizontal Arrangement

Hide Workbook Windows

1 Select workbook window to hide.

2 Click **Window** menu, then click **Hide**.

   The Workbook window disappears from view.

Unhide Workbook Window

1 Click **Window** menu, then click **Unhide**.

   The Unhide dialog box appears.

2 Select workbook to unhide, then click **OK**.

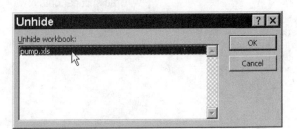

Worksheet Window Commands

To view different parts of a large worksheet at one time, you can use the Split command to create separate panes that scroll independently of each other. To keep headings or titles in view as you scroll down or across a worksheet, you can use the Freeze Panes command.

Window ➡ Split / Freeze Panes

Notes:

- In **step 1**, the split will occur above and to the left of the selected cell. Therefore, you can split a worksheet into as many as four panes, each with its own set of scroll bars.

- To split the worksheet horizontally, select a cell in column A.

  When you split a window horizontally, the panes scroll together when you scroll left and right, but they scroll independently when you scroll up and down.

- To split worksheet vertically, select a cell in row 1.

  When you split a window vertically, the panes scroll together when you scroll up or down, but each pane scrolls independently when you scroll left and right.

- When you **freeze a pane** *(see next page)*, the top and/or left panes lock when you scroll through the worksheet.

Split Worksheet Window Into Panes

1 Select cell to indicate row and column where split will take place.

2 Click **Window** menu, then click **Split**.

   Excel divides worksheet into two or four panes.
   Each pane contains its own set of scroll bars.

market35.xls						
	A	B	C	D	E	F	G
1				MICHAEL CRAWFORD			
2				STOCK ANALYSIS - TRANSACTIONS FOR 199-			
3							
4	NO. OF	COMPANY		DATE	DATE	SELLING	
5	SHARES	NAME	SYMBOL	BOUGHT	SOLD	PRICE	COST
6	200	Crystal Motors	CM	1/15/96	11/5/96	6548.95	7453
7	100	US Brands	USB	1/30/96	6/30/96	9057.43	6923
8	50	IGM	IGM	2/17/96	4/25/96	3248.95	2576
9	300	Microgem	MIG	2/17/96	12/5/96	3954.69	539
111		Named Ranges	References				
112		PRINTALL	=Sheet1!$A$1:$J$12				
113		STOCK	=Sheet1!$A$1:$B$12				
114		Totals	=Sheet1!$C$12:$J$12				

Sheet1 / Sheet2 / Sheet3 / Sheet4 / Sheet5 / Sheet6

Ready · NUM

Adjust or Remove Panes

1 Point to split bar.

   Pointer becomes double-arrow.

2 Drag split bar to move it.

   To remove the split bar:

   • Drag spilt bar onto row or column headings.

118

- When you freeze panes, you cannot change their location by dragging a split bar. Instead you must unfreeze the panes, then reset them by dragging a split bar, or by selecting a new starting cell.

Freeze Panes

Locks top and/or upper-left pane created at location indicated by your selection, or locks these panes created by split proce-dure (see previous page).

1 Select cell to indicate row and column
   where split will take place.

   *NOTE: Skip step 1, if you have already split the
             window into panes (previous page).*

2 Click **Window** menu, then click **Freeze Panes**.

   *Excel divides worksheet into two or four panes.
   There is only one set of scroll bars, as the top and/or
   left panes are frozen and will not scroll.*

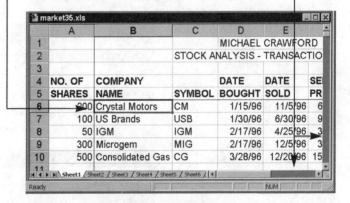

frozen
area

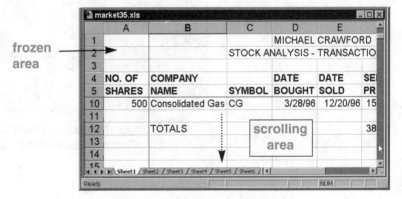

Unfreeze Panes

- Click **Window** menu, then click **Unfreeze Panes**.

Undo and Repeat Actions

Excel lets you undo not only your last action but a series of actions. Then, if you change your mind again, Excel lets you repeat the actions you have undone.

Edit ➔ ↰ Undo / ↻ Repeat

Notes:

- You can press **Ctrl+Z** to quickly undo your last action.

- You can press **Ctrl+Y** to quickly repeat your last action.

- Excel maintains a history of actions and repeated actions for all open workbooks.

Undo or Repeat Last Action Using Menu

1 Click **Edit** menu.

The edit menu displays possible undo and repeat actions.

2 Click **Undo** *action* to undo the last action.

OR

Click **Repeat** *action* to repeat the last action.

NOTE: Repeated actions do not have to be carried out on the same cell or object.

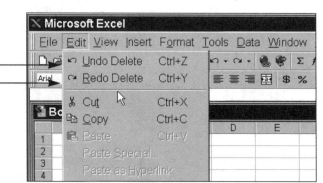

Undo Delete and Redo Delete Commands on Edit Menu

Tip: To undo a cell entry before completing it, press Esc. If you have already completed the entry in a cell, press Ctrl+Z (Undo).

120

Undo Last Actions Using Toolbar

1 Click arrow of **Undo** button on Standard toolbar.

Excel opens a drop-down list of past actions.

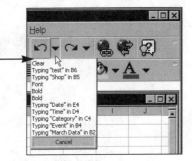

2 Click first action on list.

OR

Move pointer through series of actions to undo, then click.

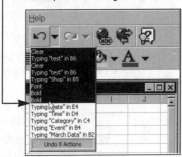

Repeat Last Actions Using Toolbar

1 Click arrow of **Redo** button on Standard toolbar.

Excel opens a drop-down list of undone actions.

2 Click first action on list.

OR

Move pointer through series of actions to repeat, then click.

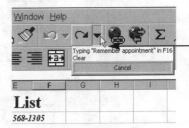

Validate Cell Entries

You can use the Validate feature to make sure that only correct data is entered in your worksheet. For example, you can restrict the entry in a cell to whole numbers and provide prompts for the user. When an incorrect entry is made, you can specify the kind of error message to display.

Data ➡ Validation...

Notes:

- In **step 1**, select multiple cells only if the restriction you are setting will apply equally to all the cells.

- In **step 5**, comparison operators include: *between, not between, equal to, not equal to, greater than, less than, greater than or equal to, less than or equal to.*

- Option: Select **Ignore blank** to permit referenced cells (step 6) to be blank.

- Data validation options in the **Allow** box in **step 4** include:

  Any value — use to let cell accept any value.

  Whole number — use to restrict entries to values that are not decimal numbers.

  decimal — use to restrict entries to values that include decimal values.

  continued...

Restrict Cell Entries of Numbers, Dates, or Times

1. Select cell(s) to restrict.
2. Click **Data** menu, then click **Validate**.
   The Data Validation dialog box appears.
3. Click **Settings** tab.
4. Select one of the following data types in the **Allow** box:
   Whole Number, Decimal, Date, Time
5. Select desired comparison operator in **Data** box.
6. Set data restriction in the **Value**, **Minimum**, **Maximum** boxes.
   You can enter values, cell references, or formulas in these boxes.

   NOTE: *The boxes that appear will depend on the comparison operator you select in step 5.*

7. Set **Input Message** for restricted cells as shown in the illustration on the next page.
8. Set **Error Message** for restricted cells as shown in the illustration on the next page.
9. Set other options described in the notes on the left, then click **OK**.

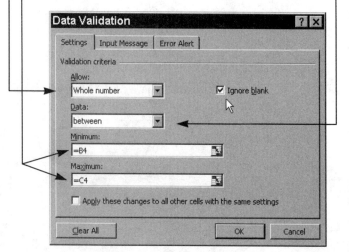

List — use to restrict entries to items contained in a list (a range of cells containing text or numbers).

Date — use to restrict entries to a valid date or range of dates.

Time — use to restrict entries to a valid time or range of times.

Text length — use to specify the number of valid characters in an entry.

Custom — use to restrict entries to one that causes a formula to evaluate to True. For example, if you specify that an entry in A1 is equal to an entry in B3 as in this logical formula: =A1=B3.

Set Input and Error Message for Restricted Cells

1 Click the **Input Message** tab, and type the title and input message as shown in the example below.

2 Click the **Error Alert** tab, and type title and message as shown below, then click **OK** when done.

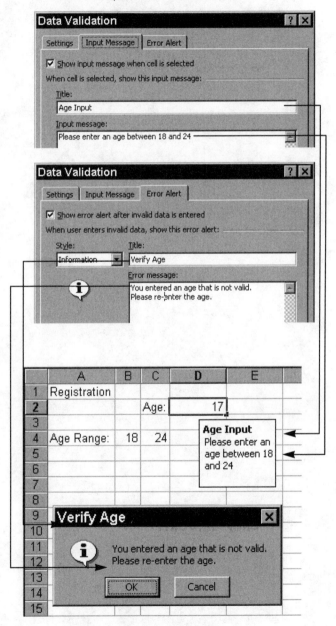

Validation and Message Settings

123

Formulas, Lists, and Data Tables

This section contains illustrated procedures arranged in alphabetical order for creating and working with formulas, lists, and data tables.

About Formulas

You will enter and build formulas to calculate values stored in your worksheet. Here, you will receive basic information about formulas — formula location, formula parts, controlling the order of operation, and formula examples. For additional information, see *About References in Formulas, Create Formulas, Create Functions,* and *Edit Formulas.*

Notes:

- A **formula** is an instruction to calculate numbers.

- You can set Excel to display formulas in cells: Click **Tools** menu, then **Options**; click the **View** tab, and select the **Formulas** Window option.

Formula Location

You will enter a formula in the cell where the result should appear. As you type the formula, it appears in the cell and in the formula bar. After you enter a formula, the result is displayed in the cell, and the formula is displayed in the formula bar. *(See Create Formulas for details.)*

formula ———→

formula result ———→

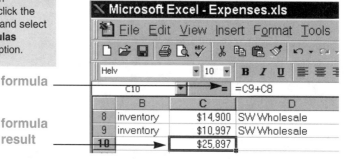

Notes:

- **References** and **reference names** indicate the location of cells in a worksheet.

- **Functions** are predefined formulas that use arguments in fixed locations to perform calculations.

- **Operators** tell Excel the kind of calculation to perform.

- **Parentheses** affect the order of operations and must be used in pairs.

Formula Parts

Formulas always begin with an equal sign (=) and often contain the elements shown in bold type in the following sample formulas:

numbers	=A1+**25**
cell references	=**A1**-25
reference names	=A1***Salary**
functions	=**Sum(A1:A10)**+Salary
operators	=A1**/**2**+**25***22**-**3
parentheses	=**(**24+A1**)**/2**%**

Notes:

- When a formula contains both an addition and subtraction operator, Excel performs the operations from left to right.

Control the Order of Operations in Formulas

It is important to consider the order of mathematical operations when preparing formulas. Excel will perform the operation in your formulas in the following order:

- operations enclosed in parentheses ( )
- percentage %
- exponential ^
- multiplication and division * /
- addition and subtraction + -
- concatenation (connection of text strings) &
- comparisons = < > <= >= <>

Notes:

- Some of the examples contain named references. You must first name a range, before you can refer to its name in a formula. However, Excel will let you use names automatically when labels exist next to numbers in your worksheet.

Formula Examples

This is a list of common formulas followed by a brief explanation:

=A1+25 — adds the contents of cell A1 to the constant 25.

=A1-25 — from the content of cell A1, subtracts 25.

=A1*TotalSalary — multiplies the content of cell A1 by the content of the cell named TotalSalary.

=Sum(A1:A10)+TotalSalary — adds the content of the cell named TotalSalary to the sum of the range of cells A1 through A10.

=A10+(25*TotalSalary) — multiplies the content of the cell named TotalSalary by 25, then adds that to the content of cell A10.

=A10^3 — multiplies the content of A10 by itself 3 times (exponentially).

=2%*A10 — two percent of the content of cell A10.

=(Min(Salary)+Max(Salary))/2 — adds the minimum value in the range of cells named Salary to the maximum value in that range, and divides it by 2.

=A10 & " " & A11 — combines the text in cells A10 and A11 with a space between them. If A10 contains HELLO and A11 contains THERE, the result would be HELLO THERE.

=IF(A1<>0,A1*B10," ") — If value in cell A1 is not zero, multiplies A1 by value in B10, otherwise displays blank text.

About References in Formulas

References are cell locations in your worksheet. You will often insert references in formulas to indicate the locations of values you want the formula to calculate. For additional information, see *About Formulas*, *Create Formulas*, *Create Functions*, and *Edit Formulas*.

Notes:

- A **reference** is a notation that identifies the location of a cell in a workbook.

- A **range** is a group of consecutive cells.

- A **union** combines multiple references into one reference.

- An **intersection** of ranges indicates where two ranges meet.

- A **named reference** indicates a cell or range to which you have assigned a name.

- A **reference to other worksheets** requires an exclamation sign to separate the sheet name from the cell reference. Quotation marks are needed if worksheet names contain spaces.

- **3-D references** identify a range of cells in different worksheets that are in the same position on each sheet.

- **External references** require the drive and folder locations. Quotation marks are needed if file names contains spaces.

References — Cell Locations

References are a way to indicate the location of a cell or range of cells in a formula. Here is a list of the kinds of references you can use. Range operators in example references are bolded.

REFERENCE TYPE	EXAMPLE
range	A1**:**A10
union of cells	C5**,**E5
intersection (space)	C5:C10 **A7:E7**
entire column	C**:**C
entire row	3**:**3
range of columns	A**:**C
range of rows	3**:**5
named reference	TotalSalary
cells in another worksheet	Sheet2**!**A10
3-D range of cells	Sheet1**:**Sheet3**!**A10
external reference (link) to cells in another workbook	'c:\my docs\[sales.xls]!Sheet1'!A10

Notes:

- The type of reference becomes important when you copy or move formulas.

  For example, it is common to copy formulas down a column that refer to cells in the same row. In this case, the relative references will adjust appropriately. If the same formula contains a reference to a value that is not moved, errors will occur after you copy the formulas, unless you have created an absolute reference to that cell.

Reference Types

Relative Cell Reference

A **relative cell reference** (such as A2) describes a cell location that is not fixed when the formula is moved or copied.

Formula example: =A2*10

If this cell is copied one cell down, the reference A2 would become A3. Thus the copied formula would become =A3*10

Absolute Cell Reference

An **absolute cell reference** (such as $A$2) describes a cell that will not change when the formula is moved or copied. Use a dollar sign ($) before both the column letter and the row number to specify an absolute cell reference.

Formula example: =$A$2*10

If this cell is copied one cell down, the reference A2 would remain $A$2. Thus the copied formula would remain =$A$2*10

Mixed Cell Reference

A mixed cell reference (such as $A2) describes a cell location with relative and absolute parts. The dollar sign ($) marks the absolute part of the reference (A), while the unmarked part (2) defines the relative part of the reference.

Formula example: =$A2*10

If this cell is copied one cell down and one cell position to the right, only the relative part of the reference will adjust. Thus the copied formula would become =$A$3*10

Notes:

- In **step 2**, you can click anywhere on reference to change.

- When you first press **F4**, Excel selects and changes the reference. Keep pressing **F4** until the desired reference type appears.

Change Reference Type

1 Double-click formula containing reference to change.

2 Click on reference to change.

3 Press **F4** until desired reference type appears.

4 Press **Enter**.

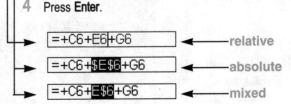

=+C6+E6+G6 ← relative

=+C6+$E$6+G6 ← absolute

=+C6+E$6+G6 ← mixed

Audit Formulas in Worksheets

If you have an error or unexpected result in a formula, you may wish to audit or trace the formula to determine the source of the problem. For this purpose, Excel provides the Auditing toolbar. Also see *Comments* for information about adding comments to cells, and *Validate Cell Entries* for information about how to ensure valid entries are made.

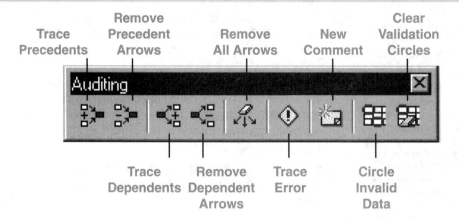

Trace Precedents	Remove Precedent Arrows	Remove All Arrows	New Comment	Clear Validation Circles

Trace Dependents	Remove Dependent Arrows	Trace Error	Circle Invalid Data

Notes:

- You can dock the floating Auditing toolbar by dragging it to top or bottom of the Excel window.

Display Auditing Toolbar

1 Click **View** menu, then point to or click **Toolbars**.

2 Click **Customize** on the submenu that appears.

The Customize dialog box appears.

3 Click the **Toolbars** tab, select **Auditing,** and click **Close**.

Notes:

- **Dependents** are cells containing formulas that refer to the cell you want to audit.

Trace Dependents

1 Select cell to trace.

2 Click **Trace Dependents** button on Auditing toolbar.

Excel draws arrows to formulas that refer to cell.

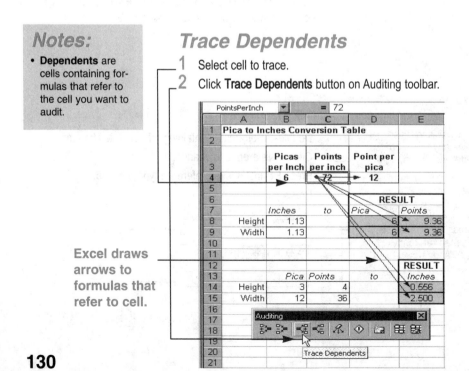

Trace Precedents

1 Select cells containing formula to analyze.

2 Click **Trace Precedents** button on Auditing toolbar.

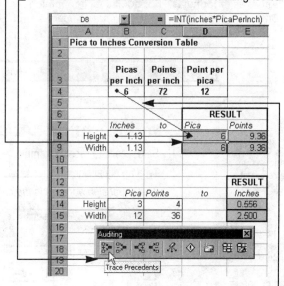

Excel draws arrows to cells formula refers to.

Trace Errors

1 Select cells containing error to analyze.

2 Click **Trace Errors** button on Auditing toolbar.

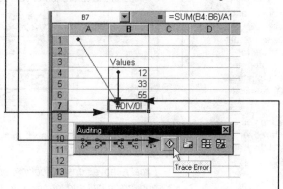

Excel draws arrows to source of error.

Create Formulas (Simple)

You will enter and build formulas to calculate values stored in your worksheet. Here, you will receive basic information about building formulas, pasting names into a formula, and inserting references in formulas. For additional information, see *About References in Formulas*, *Create Formulas (Complex)*, *Create Functions*, and *Edit Formulas*.

Notes:

- In **step 1**, select a cell in which you want the result of the calculation to appear.

- In **step 2**, when you type the equal sign, controls appear on the formula bar. These controls are described on the next page.

- In the illustration, the simple formula =25*A1 multiplies the value in A1 by 25.

- You can repeat the process of inserting a reference and typing an operator until all the cells you want to calculate are included in the formula. For information about changing a formula, see *Edit Formulas*.

- If you decide you want to start over and cancel the entry, press **Esc**.

Build Formula (Add References)

1 Select cells to receive formula.

2 Type an equal sign (=).
   The equal sign appears in the cell and in the formula bar.

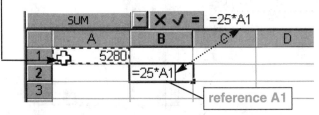

3 Type the formula *(for examples see About Formulas)*.

To insert a reference in formula by pointing:

- Click cell containing value to reference.
  A dashed line appears around the cell, and Excel inserts the reference in your formula.

4 Type next part of formula. If formula is complete, go to step 5, below.
   Excel removes dashed outline, and what you type appears in cell and formula bar.

5 Press **Enter**.
   OR
   Click ✓ on formula bar.
   Excel calculates the formula and displays the result in the cell.

Paste a Named Range into a Formula

1 Place insertion point in formula.
2 Click **Insert** menu, then click or point to **Name**.
3 Click **Paste** on the submenu that appears.
4 Click name to paste in formula, then click **OK**.

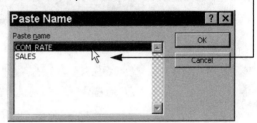

Create Formula, Insert Cell References, and Change Reference Type

1 If you wish, first type the data in a new worksheet as shown in the illustration below. Then create the typical formula in C7 that calculates the commission (=$B$2*C5).

	A	B	C	D
1		SALES COMMISSION		
2	COM RATE	4.00%		
3				
4		ELMHURST	CADDY	WUILLS
5	SALES	640000	340000	540000
6	BONUS	2000	1000	2000
7	COMMISSION	25600		
8	TOTAL COMP	27600		

2 Select cell to receive formula (C7).
3 Type **=** to start the formula.
4 Click cell to insert as reference in formula (B2).

To change the inserted reference to absolute:

- Press **F4**.

  Reference changes to absolute (B2 becomes $B$2).

5 Type desired operator (*****) .
6 Click next cell to insert as reference in formula (C5).
7 Press **Enter** to complete the formula.

Create Formulas (Complex)

In this topic you will learn the basic skills needed to create complex formulas — formulas that use simple functions containing references to a range of cells, cells in other worksheets, cells in other workbooks, and cells that span consecutive worksheets.

Notes:

- **Functions** are predefined formulas that perform specific kinds of calculations. This topic will introduce you to the **SUM function**. See *Create Functions* for more information about functions.

- In **step 2**, the SUM function requires a pair of parentheses: SUM( ). Within the parentheses, you will type or insert the cells to total. This element of a function is called an **argument**. You can use the SUM function to calculate many kinds of references, not just a range, as in this example: SUM(A1, B3, B4:B10). See *About References* for additional information.

Create SUM Function and Insert a Range by Dragging

1   Select cells to receive formula.

2   Type an equal sign (=), then type **SUM(.**
   What you type appears in the cell and in the formula bar.

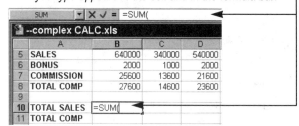

To insert a range in formula by dragging:

- Drag through cells containing values to calculate.
  A dashed line appears around the range, and Excel inserts the reference in your formula.

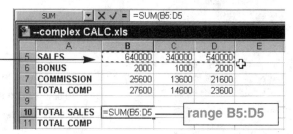

3   Type closing parentheses.
   Excel removes dashed outline, and what you type appears in cell and formula bar.

4   Press **Enter**.
   OR
   Click ✓ on formula bar.
   Excel calculates the formula and displays the result in the cell.

Notes:

- In the illustration, the external reference (or link) shown includes the name of the workbook, the sheet name, followed by the cell range. If you close the source workbook, the reference will expand to include the folder in which the workbook has been saved.

Insert an External Reference into a Formula

1 Open workbook containing cells to reference.

2 In destination worksheet, create the formula, then place insertion point in formula where external reference will be inserted.

3 Select workbook, then worksheet, then cell or range to insert.

Excel inserts external reference in formula.

4 Type next part of formula.

= =SUM([YEAREND.xls]Sheet1!$A$1:$B$1)

Notes:

- A reference to a cell or range on another worksheet starts with the sheet name separated by an exclamation point, as in these examples:

=SUM(Sheet2!B1)

=SUM(Sheet2!B1:B5)

- A reference to a range of cells that spans multiple sheets is often called a **3-D reference**.

Insert a Reference to Cells in Another Sheet or 3-D Range

1 In destination worksheet, create the formula, then place insertion point in formula where reference will be inserted.

To insert a cell or range reference on another sheet:

- Click source worksheet tab, then click cell or range to insert.

  Excel inserts worksheet reference in formula.

To insert a 3-D reference to cells in a range of worksheets:

a Click first worksheet tab in range.

b Click cell or range on that sheet to insert.

c Press **Shift** and click last sheet tab in range of sheets.

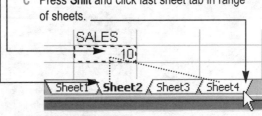

Excel inserts 3-D worksheet reference.

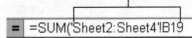

= =SUM('Sheet2:Sheet4'!B19

2 Type next part of formula.

Create Functions

Functions are predefined formulas that perform specific kinds of calculations, such as finding an average or future value. Functions require arguments — the data needed to perform the calculation. To make it easy to create a function, Excel provides the Paste Function Wizard.

Paste Function button

SUM ▼ X ✓ = =SUM(B5:B9)

Functions list on formula bar

Notes:

- You can also click the **Paste Function** button when you want to insert a function in a formula you have already started to create.

- When creating a formula, you can click the **Function list** on the formula bar to quickly insert frequently used functions and access the **Paste Function Wizard**.

- The **Paste Function Wizard** may suggest a range by inserting it in a **Number** box. Delete this range if it is not appropriate.

- As you click in **Number** boxes, the Paste Function Wizard adds more boxes.

Insert a Function Using Function Wizard

1 Select cell in which function will be created.

2 Click **Paste Function** button on Standard toolbar.

The Paste Function dialog box appears.

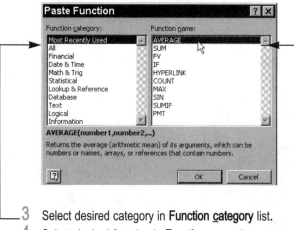

3 Select desired category in **Function category** list.

4 Select desired function in **Function name** list, then click **OK**.

A dialog box specific to the function you selected appears.

Dialog Collapse button

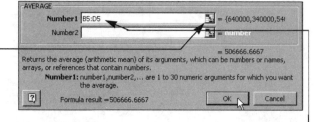

5 Insert cell references or values in **Number** boxes that appear.

   NOTE: You can click the **Collapse Dialog** button on the right side of the **Number** box, then select the cells to calculate directly from the worksheet. (See Use Dialog Box Controls.)

6 Click **OK** when done.

Notes:

- In **step 1**, if you double-click the cell, then click the **Paste Function** button, you will insert a new function into your existing function at the insertion point.
- In **step 3**, refer to illustration on bottom of previous page.

Edit a Function

1 Select cell containing the function to edit.

   NOTE: Do not double-click the cell.

2 Click the **Paste Function** button on Standard toolbar.

3 Change arguments in **Number** boxes as desired, then click **OK**.

Notes:

- For this procedure, refer to illustrations on the previous page.
- A **nested function** is a function that contains a function as an argument.

Combine (Nest) Functions

1 Double-click cell containing function(s).

2 Place insertion point where new function will be inserted, or select argument to replace with a function.

3 Click the **Paste Function** button on Standard toolbar.

4 Select desired category in **Function category**.

5 Select desired function in **Function name** list, then click **OK**.

6 Insert cell references or values in **Number** boxes that appear.

7 Click **OK** when done.

$$=AVERAGE(B5:B9,SUM(B6:D6))$$

Nested Functions

Notes:

- If Excel detects subtotals within a range of values, it may suggest to add just those totals to obtain a grand total. When this happens, Excel applies dashed outlines only to the cells containing subtotals in the immediate column or row.

Use AutoSum Function

1 Click cell to receive the function.

2 Click **AutoSum** button on Standard toolbar.

   Excel suggests cells to add with dashed outline.

3 To change the proposed range, drag through desired cells.

4 Press **Enter** when done.

	A	B	C	D	E
4		ELMHURST	CADDY	TOTALS	
5	SALES	640000	340000	=SUM(B5:C5)	
6	BONUS	2000	1000		

137

Create Lookup Tables

You can create a table, then utilize Excel's built-in lookup functions, VLOOKUP and HLOOKUP, to find particular values in the table and display them in a cell. For example, you can use VLOOKUP to look up information about the status of a flight by simply typing in the flight number.

VLOOKUP ▼ X ✓ = =VLOOKUP($A$4,TABLE,2)

Notes:

- In **step 1**, be sure the table does not include blank rows. The first column should contain the lookup values (flight numbers in the example), which may be text, values, or references to other cells.

- **Step 2** is optional, but recommended. To name the table, select it, then click in the name box and type the desired name. For additional information, see *Name Cells*.

- In **step 3**, it is best to set up this area above the table, to avoid having to move it when the table of information grows.

- Use VLOOKUP when records in table are organized in rows.

- Use HLOOKUP when records in table are organized in columns. This organization is not typical for data in lists.

Use VLOOKUP to Return Information Stored in a Table

Refer to the step numbers in the example on the next page when executing these steps.

1 Create the table of information, such as the list of flights shown in the illustration.

2 Select the table and name it, such as TABLE.

3 Type labels to identify where information returned by VLOOKUP will appear.

4 Type initial value to be found, (211 in example), in blank cell under appropriate label, (Flight No. in example).

5 Select cell to return information.

6 Type **=VLOOKUP(**

7 Select cell in which you typed the look up value to find, to insert its cell reference in the formula (A4 in example).

8 Type the remainder of the function: **,TABLE,2, False)**

=VLOOKUP(*A4,TABLE,2,False*)

A4 . . . . Indicates cell containing value to look up.

, (commas) . . . . Separate each argument.

TABLE . . . . Refers to name of range containing information.

2 . . . . Indicates column number in table containing information to return.

False . . . . An optional argument that tells Excel to find an exact match.

9 Press **Enter**.

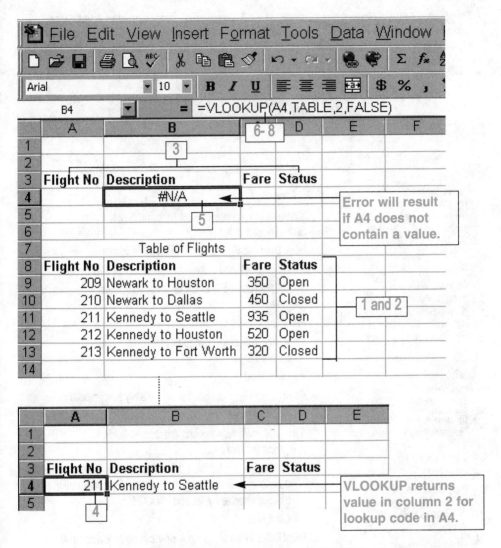

Find Flight Information Using VLOOKUP

TIP: In the example, you could create VLOOKUP
         functions under the Fare and Status labels to
         return information in columns 3 and 4, respec-
         tively, for lookup values typed in cell A4.

Create PivotTables

A PivotTable lets you interactively analyze and summarize data stored in a list. For example, it can show subtotals for expense categories for all vendors, or just a particular vendor. For information about changing a PivotTable and its views, see *Edit PivotTables*. For information about lists see *Lists*.

Data → ▣ PivotTable Report...

Notes:

- A **list** (or database) must contain labels that define **field names** so Excel can determine the categories of the data in the list *(see Lists)*.

- In **step 3**, Excel selects the range automatically, if you selected any cell in the list in step 1. For information about selecting a range in a dialog box, see *Use Dialog Box Controls*.

- In **step 4**, the layout diagram has the following areas that let you construct the PivotTable:

  PAGE — lets you filter the completed PivotTable by items in field.

  ROW — creates row labels for each unique item in field.

  COLUMN — creates column labels for each unique item in field.

  DATA — summarizes data in field by function indicated on button. You must include at least one field in the Data area.

Create a PivotTable from an Existing List

1   If necessary, create the list to summarize, then click any cell in list.

2   Click **Data** menu, then click **PivotTable Report**.
    PivotTable Wizard - Step 1 of 4 dialog box appears.

3   Select **Microsoft Excel list or database**, then click **Next >** .
    PivotTable Wizard - Step 2 of 4 dialog box appears.

    - If the suggested range is not correct, select a new range.
    - Click **Next >**.
    PivotTable Wizard - Step 3 of 4 dialog box appears.

4   Drag field buttons onto appropriate areas of layout diagram.
    Excel automatically assigns function to fields you place in Data area.

    - To change the function that will summarize the data fields, double-click field button, then select desired function from the **Summarize by** list and click **OK**.
    - Click **Next >**.
    PivotTable Wizard - Step 4 of 4 dialog box appears.

5   Select **New worksheet**, or **Existing Worksheet** to indicate placement of PivotTable.

    - If you selected **Existing Worksheet**, type or select in worksheet the desired cell location.
    - Click **Finish**.
    Excel creates the PivotTable based on your choices and the data in the list.

Tip: It's a good idea to limit the number of fields in a PivotTable. If necessary, create additional PivotTables to analyze your list in new ways.

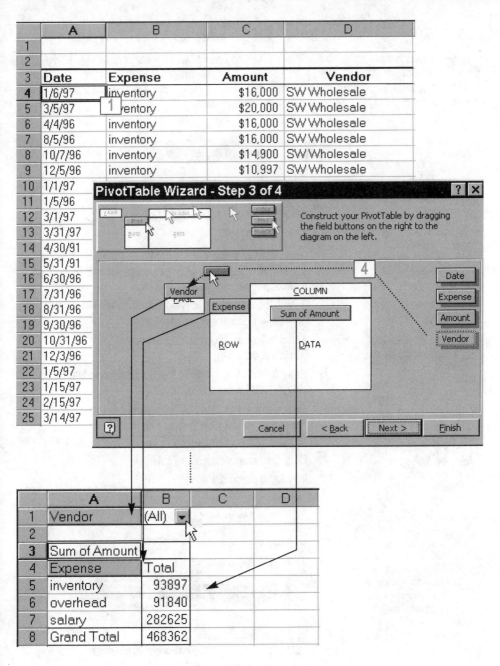

	A	B	C	D
1				
2				
3	**Date**	**Expense**	**Amount**	**Vendor**
4	1/6/97	inventory	$16,000	SW Wholesale
5	3/5/97	entory	$20,000	SW Wholesale
6	4/4/96	inventory	$16,000	SW Wholesale
7	8/5/96	inventory	$16,000	SW Wholesale
8	10/7/96	inventory	$14,900	SW Wholesale
9	12/5/96	inventory	$10,997	SW Wholesale
10	1/1/97			
11	1/5/96			
12	3/1/97			
13	3/31/97			
14	4/30/91			
15	5/31/91			
16	6/30/96			
17	7/31/96			
18	8/31/96			
19	9/30/96			
20	10/31/96			
21	12/3/96			
22	1/5/97			
23	1/15/97			
24	2/15/97			
25	3/14/97			

PivotTable Wizard - Step 3 of 4

Construct your PivotTable by dragging the field buttons on the right to the diagram on the left.

Date
Expense
Amount
Vendor

Vendor
PAGE
COLUMN
Expense
Sum of Amount
ROW
DATA

Cancel | < Back | Next > | Finish

	A	B	C	D
1	Vendor	(All) ▼		
2				
3	Sum of Amount			
4	Expense	Total		
5	inventory	93897		
6	overhead	91840		
7	salary	282625		
8	Grand Total	468362		

PivotTable Result

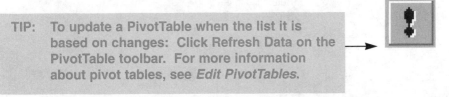

TIP: To update a PivotTable when the list it is
        based on changes: Click Refresh Data on the
        PivotTable toolbar. For more information
        about pivot tables, see *Edit PivotTables*.

Create One-Variable Data Tables

You can create a data table to generate a series of answers for a set of values organized in a column or row. You might use this feature to generate a table that converts fahrenheit to centigrade, or meters to feet. The elegance of data tables is that they achieve all the results from a single formula that calculates an array.

Data ➡ Table...

Notes:

- In **step 1**, consider typing the first two values, then fill the remaining cells by dragging the fill handle.

- In **step 3**, the formula must refer to the first column input cell that you will again refer to in step 6 below.

- In **step 4**, just select the substitution values and the cells in which the results will appear. Do not include labels that you may have typed to describe the values.

- In **step 6**, select the **Column input cell** box, if your substitution values are organized in a column. If your substitution values are organized in a row, choose the **Row input cell** box instead.

Create a One-Variable Data Table

This procedure refers to the illustration on the right. You can, of course, easily substitute your own values and formula to create a table that returns different results.

1   Type substitution values (values to substitute in formula) in a column, as shown on the right.

2   Select cell where first result will appear (C6 in the example).

3   Enter formula that refers to first substitution value (=SQRT(*B6*) in the example).

4   Select entire data table, including first column input cell, substitution values, and result cells (B6:C21 in the example).

5   Click **Data** menu, then click **Table**.
The Table dialog box appears.

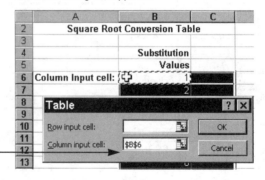

6   Click in **Column input cell** box, then click cell containing column input value (B6 in the example) to insert that reference in the box.

7   Click **OK**.

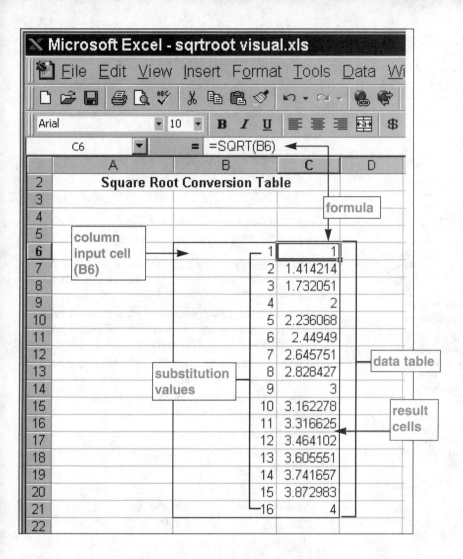

Notes:

- In **step 1**, you do not have to select the cell containing the formula.

Delete Results in a Data Table

If you attempt to delete part of the results in a data table, you will receive this message: Cannot change part of a table.

1 Select all result cells.

2 Press **Delete** key.

Create Two-Variable Data Tables ·

You can create a data table to generate a series of answers from two sets of values organized in a column and a row. You might use this feature to generate a table that calculates monthly payments for principals over different lengths of time.

Data ➝ Table...

Notes:

- In **step 1**, the row and **column input cells** refer to initial values used in the formula that correspond to substitution values in the table.

  The row input cell should contain a value used in the row of substitute numbers in the table; the column input cell should contain a value used in the column of substitution numbers in the table.

- In **step 4**, just select the substitution values and the cells in which the results will appear. Do not include labels in your selection that you may have typed to describe the values.

Create a Two-Variable Data Table

This procedure refers to the illustration on the right. You can, of course, easily substitute your own values and formula to create a table that returns different results.

1 Enter table substitution values (values to substitute in formulas) in a column and row, as shown on the right (principal values and years in the example).

   Enter row and column input values outside of the table (B16 and B17 in the example).

2 Select cell where substitution values intersect (B5 in the example).

3 Enter formula. The formula must refer to:

   row and column input cells (bolded in example below).

   =PMT(B3/12,**B17***12,-**B16**)

4 Select entire data table, including cell containing the formula (B5:F13 in the example).

5 Click **Data** menu, then click **Table**.

   The Table dialog box appears.

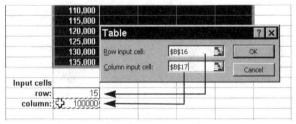

6 In **Row input cell** and **Column input cell** boxes, insert references to row and column input cells respectively.

7 Click **OK**.

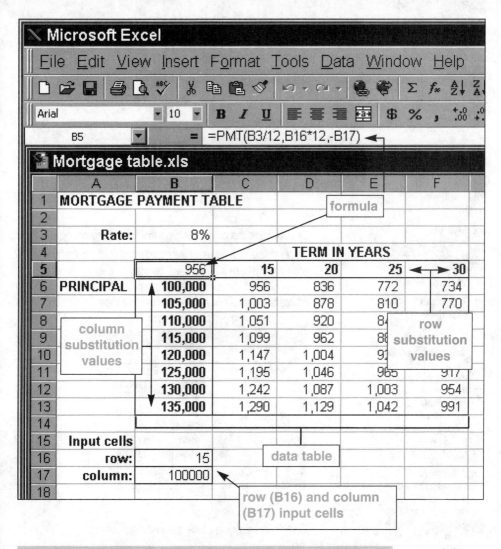

TIP: When possible, create formulas that refer to values in cells, instead of typing the value in the formula. This makes it easier to change the value. In the example, you only need to change 8% (in cell B3) to obtain a new set of results.

Notes:

- In **step 1**, you do not have to select the cell containing the formula.

Delete Results in a Data Table

If you attempt to delete part of the results in a data table, you will receive this message: Cannot change part of a table.

1 Select all result cells.
2 Press **Delete** key.

Edit Formulas

You will sometimes need to change a formula — perhaps replace an operator, add a set of parentheses, or change a cell or range the formula refers to.

- After you double-click the cell, Excel displays the formula in the cell and on the formula bar.

- To insert a function, click desired location in formula, or select function name to replace, then click the **Functions** button to the right of the formula bar (it shows the last function selected), then follow the prompts to complete the function.

- If the result achieved by editing the formula is incorrect, you can click **Edit** menu, then **Undo Typing** to undo your change.

Edit Formulas

1 Double-click the cell containing the formula to change.

Excel displays a flashing insertion pointer in the formula indicating where changes will be made. Cell references in the formula are colored, and cell outlines indicate locations of references in worksheet.

	A	B	C	Exp
2			Sales	
3		1991	35000	
4		1992	40000	
5		1993	300000	
6		1994	35000	
7		1995	39000	
8		1996	43000	
9				
10		Totals	=SUM(C4:C9)	
11				

editcalcs.xls — AVERAGE ▼ X ✓ = =SUM(C4:C9)

2 Click in the entry to place the insertion pointer.

OR

Drag through characters to select (next action will replace or delete your selection).

3 Edit the entry as needed:

- Type characters to insert.
- Press **Del** to delete characters to the right of insertion pointer or to delete the selection.
- Press **Backspace** to delete characters to the left of the insertion pointer or to delete the selection.
- Follow steps described on the next page to change reference or extend a cell range.

4 Press **Enter** or click ✓ on formula bar.

OR

To cancel the change:

Press **Esc**, or click ✗ on formula bar.

Notes:

- Excel assigns a color to each border and reference to help you identify them.

Change Reference in Formula

1 Double-click the formula to change.

Excel outlines references in worksheet with colored borders.

2 Point to border of outlined reference in worksheet.

Pointer becomes an arrow when positioned correctly.

3 Drag outline to desired cell or range.

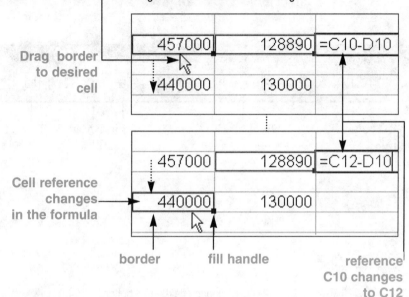

Drag border to desired cell

457000	128890	=C10-D10
440000	130000	

Cell reference changes in the formula

457000	128890	=C12-D10
440000	130000	

border   fill handle   reference C10 changes to C12

Notes:

- In **step 2**, Excel changes pointer to a crosshair to indicate that you can drag it to extend the range.

Extend Cell Range in Formula

1 Double-click the formula to change.

Excel outlines references in worksheet with colored borders.

2 Point to fill handle of outlined reference in worksheet.

Pointer becomes a crosshair when positioned correctly.

3 Drag fill handle in direction to extend the range.

40000	20000
300000	15000
35000	33000
39000	25890
43000	35000

=SUM(C4:C8)

40000	20000
300000	15000
35000	33000
39000	25890
43000	35000

=SUM(C4:D8)

Range C4:C8 becomes . . .   C4:D8

147

Edit PivotTables

Once you create a PivotTable *(see Create PivotTables)*, you can use controls in the PivotTable, such as the Page button, to filter and summarize data, or you can drag fields and items to reorganize the view of the data. Finally, you can use tools on the PivotTable toolbar to work with your table.

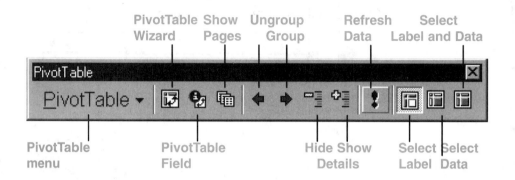

PivotTable Wizard | Show Pages | Ungroup Group | Refresh Data | Select Label and Data

PivotTable menu | PivotTable Field | Hide Show Details | Select Label | Select Data

Tip: To quickly show or hide the PivotTable toolbar, right-click any toolbar, then click PivotTable

Notes:

- In **step 1**, the page button will open to show each unique item in the field.
- **To display all page items**, repeat step 1 and select (All) from the page list.

Filter Items in PivotTable

1 Click page field arrow button.   (All) ▼
2 Click desired item in list.

Vendor	AR Office ▼
Sum of Amount	
Expense	Total
overhead	45000
office furniture	15000
Grand Total	60000

PivotTable summarizes only expenses from AR Office

Notes:

- You can undo mouse actions performed on a PivotTable: Click **Edit** menu, then click **Undo Pivot**.

Move or Remove Fields

- In PivotTable, drag field button onto desired area of table, or off PivotTable to remove it.

  As you drag button, pointer indicates action as follows:

Move to column | Move to row | Move to page | Remove

148

- In **step 1**, you can identify the cells containing summary names by words like "Sum of" and "Count of."

- You can also modify a PivotTable by selecting any cell in the table and clicking **PivotTable Wizard** on the PivotTable toolbar.

- To quickly format your PivotTable, use the AutoFormat feature *(see Format Data Tables Automatically)*.

- To delete fields from the **PivotTable Field** dialog box, click **Delete**.

- To format the number style from the **PivotTable Field** dialog box, click **Number**.

- To change the name of the summary field from the **PivotTable Field** dialog box, type a new name in the **Name** box.

Modify Summary Fields

1 Click any cell containing summary name.

Excel highlights all rows for the summarized field.

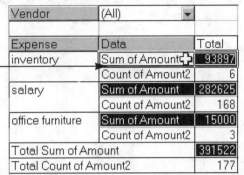

2 Click **PivotTable Field** button on PivotTable toolbar.

The PivotTable Field dialog box appears.

3 Click desired function in **Summarize by** list.

4 Click **OK** when done.

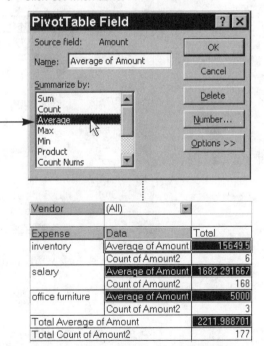

Average of Amount

149

Filter Lists Automatically

With the AutoFilter feature you can instantly display just the information you want in a list. For example, in a list containing all your company's expenses, you can show just salary or office expenses. This feature is easy to use and powerful. For information about setting up a list, see *Lists*.

Notes:

- A **list** (or database) must contain labels that define **field names**, so Excel can determine the categories of the data in the list *(see Lists)*.

- In a list, each row of information is considered a **record**. Initially, all records are displayed when you start AutoFilter.

- You can use AutoFilter with one list in a worksheet at a time. To filter multiple lists simultaneously, set up each list on a separate worksheet.

Start AutoFilter

1 Select any cell in list.

2 Click **Data** menu, then point to or click **Filter**.

3 Click **AutoFilter** on the submenu that appears.

Excel adds AutoFilter arrows to each field name in your

	A	field names	C	
1				
2				
3	**Date** ▾	**Expense** ▾	**Amount** ▾	
4	1/6/97	inventory	$16,000	SW Wh
5	3/5/97	inventory	$20,000	SW Wh
6	4/4/96	inventory	$16,000	SW Wh
7	8/5/96	inventory	$16,000	SW Wh
8	10/7/96	inventory	$14,900	SW Wh
9	12/5/96	inventory	$10,997	SW Wh
10	1/1/97	overhead	$1,000	A.B. Pro
11	1/5/96	overhead	$1,000	A.B. Pro
12	3/1/97	overhead	$1,000	A.B. Pro
13	3/31/97	overhead	$1,000	A.B. Pro
14	4/30/91	overhead	$1,000	A.B. Pro
15	5/31/91	overhead	$1,000	A.B. Pro
16	6/30/96	overhead	$1,000	A.B. Pro

AutoFilter arrow

List with AutoFilter Enabled

Notes:

- When you end AutoFilter, Excel displays all records hidden by any filters you may have selected.

End AutoFilter

1 Click **Data** menu, then point to or click **Filter**.

3 Click **AutoFilter** on the submenu that appears.

Excel removes AutoFilter arrows from each field name in your list.

For example, if you select "salary" in the Expenses field, you are selecting the criteria: Show only records that include "salary" in the Expense field.

- The **Custom** option lets you set complex criteria like: Expenses *equals* "inventory" OR Expenses *does not equal* "salary."

- The **Blanks** and **NonBlanks** options appear only if the column contains one or more blank cells.

- When you set filters for multiple columns, only records meeting both criteria are displayed.

Filter a List

1 Start AutoFilter (see previous page).

2 Click **AutoFilter arrow** of field you want to use to set the criteria.

Excel displays a list of valid criteria.

3	Date	Expense	Amount
4	1/6/97	(All)	$16,0(
5	3/5/97	(Top 10...)	$20,0(
6	4/4/96	(Custom...) inventory	$16,0(
7	8/5/96	office furniture	$16,0(
8	10/7/96	overhead	$14,9(
9	12/5/96	salary	$10,9$
10	1/1/97	(Blanks) (NonBlanks)	$1,0(
11	1/5/96	overhead	$1,0(
12	3/1/97	overhead	$1,0(

3 Click desired automatic filter option.

All: Displays all items for this field.

Top 10: Select Top/Bottom items or percent of numeric items to display.

Custom: Selects two criteria using AND or OR comparison operators.

item: Displays only records containing item you select in this field.

Blanks: Displays only records containing blank items for this field.

NonBlanks: Displays only records containing nonblank items for this field.

3	Date	Expense	Amount	Vendor
26	4/14/97	office furniture	$5,000	AR Office
27	5/14/91	office furniture	$4,000	AR Office
250				

**Blue AutoFilter arrow
indicates a filter has been
set for column.**

*Filter Shows Records with Expenses that equal "office furniture" AND
Amounts greater than $3,000*

Filter Lists (Advanced)

Advanced Filter lets you display only rows in a list that meet predefined criteria that you enter in a range of cells called the *criteria range*. For information about setting up a list, see *Lists*.

Notes:

- A **list** (or database) must contain labels that define **field names**, so Excel can determine the categories of the data in the list *(see Lists).*

- A **criterion** identifies a condition that must be met. A **criteria range** tells Excel where the criteria you typed are located in the worksheet.

Set Up a Criteria Range for Comparison Criteria

The criteria range you set up prior to using Advanced Filter tells Excel how to filter a list.

1   Insert blank rows above list you want to filter.

2   Copy column labels in the list to blank rows above the list.

> NOTE: *These labels are called **comparison labels** and they must be identical to the labels in the list you want to filter.*

3   Enter criteria below criteria labels using these guidelines:

- The criteria range cannot contain empty columns.

- To show records meeting *all* of the criteria in the criteria range, enter criteria in same row.

- To show records meeting *any* of the criteria in the criteria range, enter criteria in different rows.

- To show records meeting different criteria for the same column, set up duplicate criteria labels.

criteria range →

Region	January	
North		
	>20000	

list →

Region	January	February
North	10111	13400
South	22100	24050
East	13270	15670
West	10800	21500

result →

Region	January	February
North	10111	13400
South	22100	24050

Result of Advanced Filter Criteria Copied to Another Location

152

Criteria Examples

TO FIND:	EXAMPLE:
an exact text match	="=text to find"
any character in a specific position . . .	Topic?
consecutive characters in a . . . . specific position	Sa*y
a question mark, asterisk, or tilde	What is that~?
a value greater than another value . . .	>1000

Filter a List with Advanced Filtering

1 Set up criteria range *(see previous page)*.

2 Click **Data** menu, then point to or click **Filter**.

3 Click **Advanced Filter** on the submenu that appears.

The Advanced Filter dialog box appears.

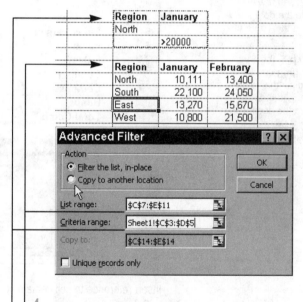

4 Insert reference to list in **List range** box.

5 Insert reference to criteria range in **Criteria range** box.

6 Select **Filter the list, in-place**.

OR

Select **Copy to another location**, then insert destination reference in **Copy to** box.

7 Click **OK**.

153

Goal Seek

The Goal Seek feature adjusts a value in a cell that you specify until a dependent formula achieves the desired goal. For example, you can use Goal Seek to find the sales needed for a sales person to achieve a total compensation of $100,000.

Tools ➡ Goal Seek...

Notes:

- In **step 1**, **dependent values** are cells in the worksheet that a formula contains references to.

- In **step 3**, the **Set cell** contains a reference that indicates the location of the formula that will calculate the goal specified in the **To value** box.

- In **step 5**, the **By changing cell** box identifies the value to change in order to obtain the desired goal.

Find a Specific Solution to a Formula with Goal Seek

1 Enter data, formula, and dependent values.

2 Click **Tools** menu, then click **Goal Seek**.

The Goal Seek dialog box appears.

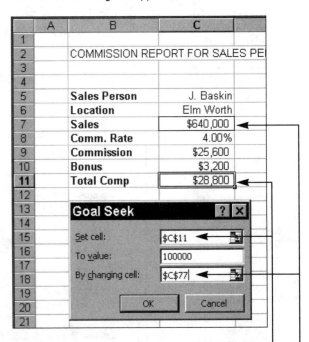

3 Insert reference to cell containing formula in **Set cell** box.

4 In the **To value** box type the goal for the formula.

5 Insert reference to cell containing value to change in the **By changing cell** box.

6 Click **Ok** when done.

continued . . .

- In **step 7**, you can click the **Step** command to move through the goal-seeking iterations one step at a time. This option will not be available if your computer performs the calculations quickly.

- **Iterations** indicate the number of times Excel will calculate a formula until a specific result or condition is met. To set limits for iterations refer to *Set Calculation Options*.

Find a Specific Solution to a Formula with Goal Seek (continued)

The Goal Seek Status dialog box appears.

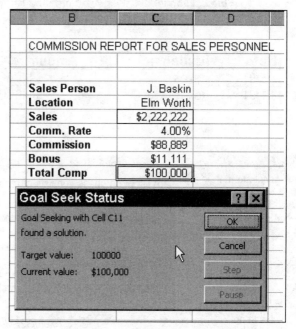

7 Click **OK** to change value to the solution found by Goal Seek.

OR

Click **Cancel** to return to original values.

TIP: Excel provides a custom program (or add-in) called Solver that you can use to solve complex what-if problems.   Solver's methods are similar to that of Goal Seek. If you installed Solver, you can click Tools menu, then Solver to run it.

Lists

Excel recognizes information organized in rows with column labels as a list (or database). Excel treats each row in a list as a record and columns as fields. Field names are derived from the column labels. Once you create a list, you can perform database tasks, such as sorting and filtering, and you can generate subtotals or PivotTables.

Date ▼	Expense ▼	Amount ▼	Vendor ▼
2/5/91	taxes	$440	City of Franklin
3/1/91	taxes	$440	City of Franklin

Notes:

- You should format **field names** differently from the records in your list.

- If field names must contain two lines, combine each line in one cell by pressing **Alt+Enter** to create a line break.

- You should not leave a blank row between the field names and the first record in a list.

- The data you type in each record of a field should be of a consistent type. That is, the data should be all values or all text. This will produce better results when performing database operations like sorting.

Parts of a List

A list or database consists of records organized in rows and columns as follows:

field names . . . . . . Identify categories of information. You indicate the field names by typing column labels.

Example: Expense, Amount

records Each row, except the first row of labels, is a record in the list.

Example: 2/5/91/ taxes, $440, City of . . .

fields . . . . Each column is a field in the list.

Example: The Expense field, the Amount field

	Date	Expense	Amount	Vendor
5				
6	Date	Expense	Amount	Vendor
7	2/5/91	taxes	$440	City of Franklin
8	3/1/91	taxes	$440	City of Franklin
9	2/5/91	taxes	$500	City of Franklin
10	1/1/97	rent	$1,000	A.B. Properti
11	1/5/96	rent	$1,000	A.B. Properti
12	3/1/97	rent	$1,000	A.B. Properti
13	3/31/97	rent	$1,000	A.B. Properties
14	3/14/97	rent	$1,000	A.B. Properties
15	3/14/97	office furniture	$3,000	AR Office
16	5/14/91		$4,000	AR Office
17	4/14/97		$5,000	AR Office
18	3/14/97		$5,000	A.B. Properties
19	4/4/96		$5,000	A.B. Properties
20	12/5/96	inventory	$10,997	SW Wholesale
21	10/7/96	inventory	$14,900	SW Wholesale
22	1/6/97	inventory	$16,000	SW Wholesale
23	4/4/96	inventory	$16,000	SW Wholesale
24	8/5/96	inventory	$16,000	SW Wholesale
25	3/5/97	inventory	$20,000	SW Wholesale
26				

field names

record (row)

field (column)

Sample List

Notes:

- When possible, store lists below data in a worksheet. This way, as the list grows it will not run into your data. Store list summary labels and formulas above the list for the same reason.

Location of Lists

Keep the following guidelines in mind when placing a list:

- If you need to store more than one list in a workbook, it is best to store each on its own worksheet.

  Reason: The AutoFilter command can only process one list in a worksheet at a time.

- Do not store other data in cells adjacent to list data.

  Reason: It becomes hard to distinguish where the list ends and other data begins.

- Avoid storing data to the left or right of a list.

  Reason: When you filter records in a list, Excel hides entire rows, including data outside the list.

Notes:

- When you insert records, Excel automatically extends references to ranges affected by the insertion.

  For example, the formula =SUM(C10:C100) would become =SUM(C10:C102) after you insert records as shown in the example to the right.

- To add a record to the end of a list: Enter new record just below last record in list.

Insert Records

1 Select records where new records will be inserted.

   NOTE: The number of records you select tells Excel how many cells to insert.

2 Right-click the selection.

3 Click **Insert** on shortcut menu that appears.

   The Insert dialog box appears.

Date	Expense	Amount	Vendor
2/5/91	taxes	$440	City of Franklin
3/1/91	taxes	$440	City of Franklin
2/5/91	taxes	$500	City of Franklin
1/1/97	rent	$1,000	A.B. Properties
1/5/96	rent	$1,000	A.B. Properties
3/1/97			roperties
3/31/97			roperties
3/14/97			roperties
3/14/97			fice
5/14/91			fice
4/14/97			fice
3/14/97			roperties
4/4/96			roperties
12/5/96	inventory	$10,997	SW Wholesale

Insert dialog box:
Insert
- ○ Shift cells right
- ● Shift cells down
- ○ Entire row
- ○ Entire column
OK   Cancel

4 Click **Shift cells down**, then click **OK**.

5 Enter new records in inserted cells.

Notes:

- In **step 1**, you can select the entire row, if you are sure that data (that might exist) to the left or right of the list will not be affected.

Delete Records

1 Select entire record.

2 Right-click the selection, then click **Delete** on shortcut menu that appears.

   The Delete dialog box appears.

3 Click **Shift cells up**, then click **OK**.

Outlines

To use the Outline feature, you must have a list containing detailed data in rows and columns, with summary rows consistently placed below the details. Once you outline a list, you can easily expand and collapse information levels to work with the data. Excel automatically outlines a list when you use the Subtotals feature.

Data ➡ Group and Outline ➡ Auto Outline

Notes:

- To clear an outline: Click **Data** menu and click **Group and Outline**, then click **Clear Outline**.

- Excel automatically outlines lists when you use the SubTotals feature. *(See Subtotal Lists Automatically.)*

Outline a List

1 Create and organize list so that related information is grouped together and summary rows are placed consistently below the details.

2 Select any cell in the list.

3 Click **Data** menu, then point to or click **Group and Outline**.

4 Click **Auto Outline** on the submenu that appears.

Outline controls appear to the left of row headings.

outline controls

details

summary rows

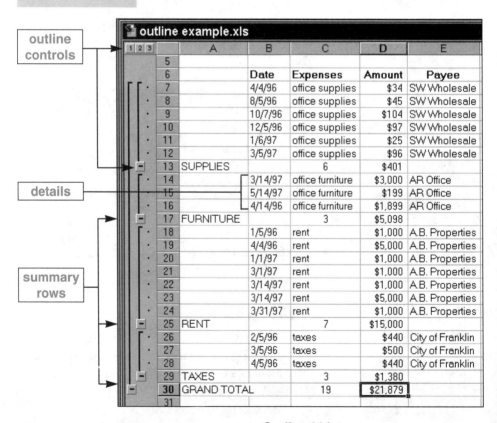

Outlined List

Collapse and Expand Outline Levels

To collapse an outline group:

- Click **Hide Detail** button.

To expand an outline group:

- Click **Show Detail** button.

To show all outline groups for a specific level:

- Click **level** button for lowest level to show.

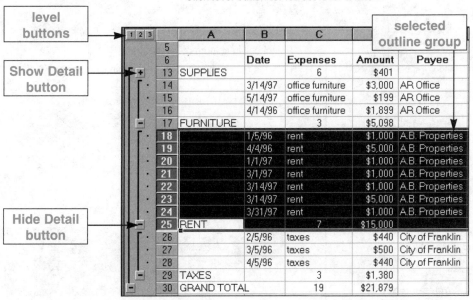

level buttons

Show Detail button

Hide Detail button

selected outline group

Example: level 2 result

159

Sort Lists

You can sort a list to arrange rows (records) in alphabetical or numerical order. Sorting groups equivalent items (such as customers from Chicago). You can arrange information in reverse alphabetical or numerical order and sort by more than one column (field), such as Lastname, then Firstname, then State.

Data ➤ ᴬ↓ Sort...

Notes:

- A **list** is a set of rows and columns that contain related data. Excel uses the labels in the first row of a list as the field names.

- In **step 1**, you must select a cell within the list that you are sorting and the column you want to sort by.

- Excel automatically detects the list and its field names. It will not include the field names in the sort.

- You can click **Edit** menu, then **Undo** to undo the sort.

- You can sort just selected cells. When you do so, Excel uses the active cell in the selection as the primary **sort key** — the field Excel sorts by.

Sort List Using Toolbar

Quickly sorts the current list by a single field (column).

1 Select cell in column of list to sort by.

2 Click the desired sort button on the Standard toolbar:

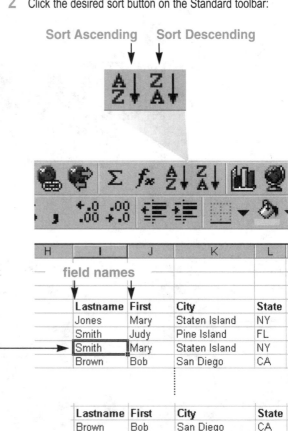

Sort Ascending   Sort Descending

field names

Lastname	First	City	State
Jones	Mary	Staten Island	NY
Smith	Judy	Pine Island	FL
Smith	Mary	Staten Island	NY
Brown	Bob	San Diego	CA

Lastname	First	City	State
Brown	Bob	San Diego	CA
Jones	Mary	Staten Island	NY
Smith	Judy	Pine Island	FL
Smith	Mary	Staten Island	NY

List Sorted (by Lastname) Using Sort Ascending Button

Notes:

- In **step 3**, the **Sort by** field is the first field (column) by which the sets of related data will be arranged. You can select two additional sort fields so that rows containing identical primary field information can be sorted further by the contents of other columns.

- To sort by more than three columns, sort the list using the least important columns. Then repeat the sort using the most important columns.

- When you sort rows that are part of an outline, Excel will keep outline families together.

Sort List Using Menu

1 Select any cell in list.

2 Click **Data** menu, then click **Sort**.
The Sort dialog box appears.

3 Select primary field to sort by in **Sort by** box.

4 Select **Ascending** or **Descending** order for the field.

To sort by multiple fields:

a Select secondary fields to sort by in **Then by** boxes.

b Select **Ascending** or **Descending** order for each field.

5 If your list does not contain field names (header row), select **No header row**.

6 Click **OK** when done.

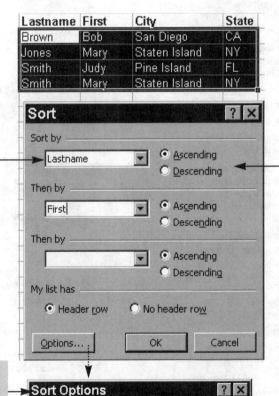

TIP: Click **Options** to select custom sort orders, change the sort orientation, or to create a case-sensitive sort order.

161

Subtotal Lists Automatically

The Subtotals feature automatically generates summary information and grand totals for information organized in a list. When you complete the Subtotals operation, Excel outlines the list and provides controls for collapsing and expanding detail levels in the list. See *Outlines* for information about using outline controls.

Data → Subtotals...

Notes:

- A **list** (or database) must contain labels that define **field names**, so Excel can determine the categories of the data in the list *(see Lists)*.

- **Field names** identify categories of information in a list.

- In a list, each row of information is considered a **record**.

- Other Subtotal options:

  Replace current subtotals — select when you do not want to create additional subtotal levels.

  Page break between groups — inserts page breaks between each group so you can print each group on a separate page.

  Summary below data — sets location of summary rows.

- You can click **Edit** menu, then **Undo Subtotals** to quickly undo the Subtotal operation.

Subtotal a List Automatically

1 Sort columns in list to subtotal *(see Sort Lists)*, then select any cell in list.

   NOTE: *Sort list by all fields you intend to subtotal.*

2 Click **Data** menu, then click **Subtotals**.

   The Subtotal dialog box appears.

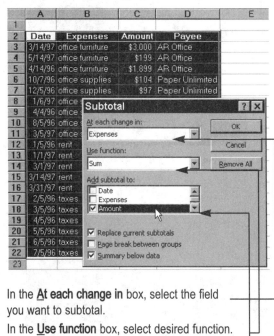

3 In the **At each change in** box, select the field you want to subtotal.

4 In the **Use function** box, select desired function.

5 In the **Add subtotal to** list, click the field name to calculate.

6 Select other options that apply *(see Notes)*.

7 Click **OK** when done.

continued . . .

Notes:

• You can press
  Ctrl+8 to hide and
  show the outline
  controls.

Subtotal a List Automatically (continued)

After you select subtotal options, Excel generates the summary rows and automatically outlines the list as shown. For information about outlines and outline controls see Outlines.

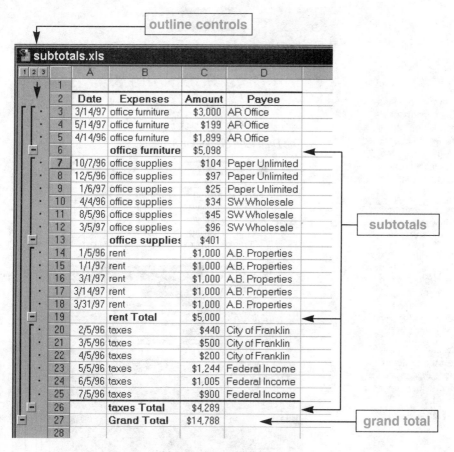

Subtotaled List

TIP: To subtotal other fields, repeat steps to Subtotal a List
       Automatically, select the field and functions, then deselect
       the Replace current subtotals option.

Notes:

• You cannot undo the
  Remove All command.

Remove Subtotals

1 Repeat steps 1 and 2 of **Subtotal a List Automatically** on
   previous page.

2 Click **Remove All**.

Use Data Forms with Lists

The Data Form feature lets you work with information stored in lists one record at a time. From a data form you can view, change, add, delete, and find records stored in the current list.

Notes:

- A **list** (or database) must contain labels that define **field names**, so Excel can determine the categories of the data in the list *(see Lists)*.

- In a list, each row of information is considered a **record**.

- A data form is particularly handy when your records span many columns. It also simplifies the process of inserting records in a list.

- You can also use the **up** and **down** arrow keys to find the previous or next record.

Open Data Form and Navigate

1 Select any cell in list.

2 Click **Data** menu, then click **Form**.
The Data form dialog box appears.

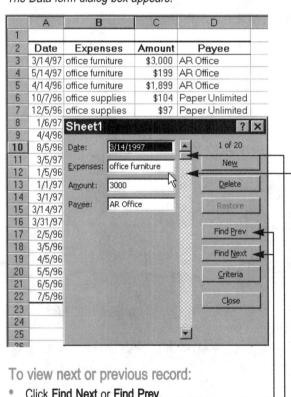

To view next or previous record:
- Click **Find Next** or **Find Prev**.

To scroll to a record:
- Drag **scroll box** up or down.

To move back or forward ten records:
- Click above or below **scroll box** on scroll bar.

3 To close the data form, click **Close** button.

Notes:

- In **step 1**, to open data form, click **Data** menu, then click **Form** (see previous page).

- In **step 2**, you can press **Tab** to quickly move to next field and select the contents of the field.

- Once you move to another record, you cannot restore a change made to a previous record.

- The **Restore** option is only available when a change has been made to a record.

Edit Records in a Data Form

1 Open the data form, then navigate to record to change.
2 Click in field box of record to change.
3 Use the usual editing techniques to change the record, such as selecting data to delete, overwriting selected data, and inserting data from the Clipboard.

To cancel changes made to current record:

- Click **Restore**. ————

4 Move to next record or click **Close** to exit.

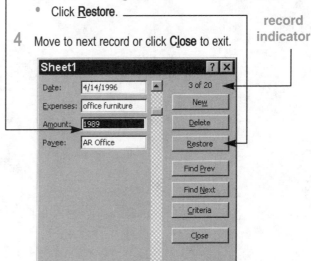

record indicator

Notes:

- In **step 3**, if you type criteria (conditions) in multiple fields, Excel will find only records that meet all of the conditions.

- In **step 4**, you can repeat this step to view all records that meet your criteria.

- Your criteria may contain wild cards and comparison operators as shown in the illustration.

- To end filtering records by your criteria, click **Criteria**, then **Clear**, then **Form**.

Find Specific Records

1 Open the data form.
2 Click **Criteria**.
3 Type criteria in field boxes.
4 Click **Find Next** or **Find Prev**.

criteria indicator

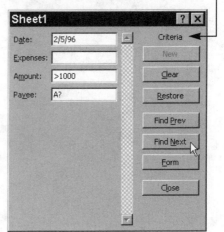

Printing and Page Setup

This section contains illustrated procedures arranged in alphabetical order, covering printing and page setup skills.

Page Breaks

Page breaks determine where worksheet pages begin and end when printing. Excel automatically creates page breaks as you work, based on the size of your worksheet, margins, scale, and other settings. However, you can insert and change page breaks to control your print results.

Insert → Page Break / Remove Page Break

View Automatic Page Breaks

1 Click **Tools** menu, then click **Options**.
The Options dialog box appears.

2 Click the **View** tab.

3 Select **Page breaks**, then click **OK**.
Dashed lines appear where pages will break when printed.

Insert Manual Page Breaks

1 Select cell, column, or row to indicate placement of page breaks.

2 Click **Insert** menu, then click **Page Break**.
Dashed lines appear where pages will break when printed, and Excel recalculates automatic page breaks for worksheet data, below and to the right of the manual page breaks.

Remove Manual Page Breaks

1 Select cell immediately to the right or below page break to remove.

OR

To remove all manual page breaks, click **Select All** button where row and column headings meet.

2 Click **Insert** menu, then click **Remove Page Break** or **Reset All Page Breaks** (if entire worksheet was selected).
Excel recalculates automatic page breaks for worksheet data.

Notes:

- While in Page Break mode, you can edit your worksheet as before.

Open Page Break Preview

This view lets you adjust page breaks with the mouse.

From Page Preview:

- Click Page Break Preview on **Page Preview** toolbar.

From the worksheet:

- Click **View** menu, then click **Page Break Preview**.

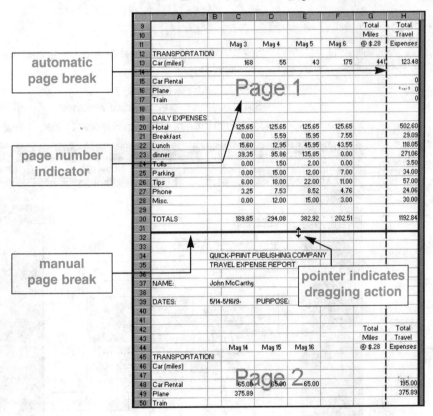

automatic page break

page number indicator

manual page break

pointer indicates dragging action

Notes:

- When you increase the area of a page by dragging a page break, Excel adjusts the scale of the printed page. *(See Set Scale and Orientation.)*

Change Page Breaks

To move a page break:

- Drag page break to desired location.

To remove a page break:

- Drag page break up or left off the print area.

169

The Print Preview feature lets you see how your worksheet will look when it's printed. From the Print Preview window you can zoom in and out, adjust margins, access the Page Setup dialog box to change settings, view other pages that will print, and print your document.

Print Preview button

Preview Your Document Before Printing It

1 Select worksheets, worksheet cells, or chart object that you intend to print.

OR

Select any cell to preview active worksheet.

2 Click **Print Preview** button on Standard toolbar.

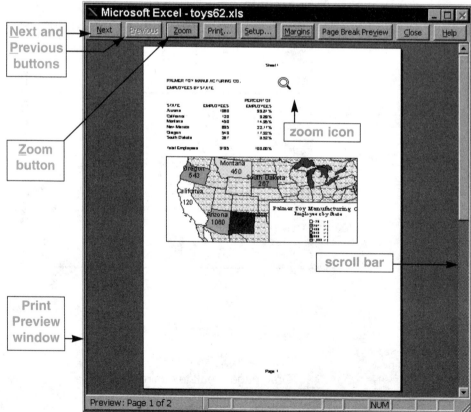

3 Click **Zoom**, then click the pointer to zoom in and out.
4 Click **Next** or **Previous** to preview other pages.
5 Click **Close** when done.

Notes:

• For information about setting margins from Print Preview see *Set Margins*.

Adjust Columns While Previewing Workbook Data

1 Click **Margins** button on Print Preview toolbar.

Margin and column handles appear in preview screen.

2 Drag a column handle to change a column dimension.

As you drag the column handle, the status bar displays the column dimension.

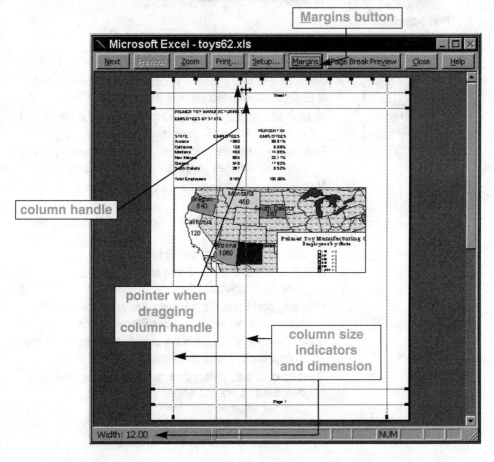

Margins button

column handle

pointer when dragging column handle

column size indicators and dimension

Notes:

• When you are done making changes from **Page Setup**, Excel will return you to the **Print Preview** window.

Change Print Settings While Previewing Workbook Data

1 Click **Setup** button on Print Preview toolbar.

The Page Setup dialog box appears.

2 Change settings as described in the the pages ahead in **Page Setup** topics:

Set Headers and Footers, Set Margins, Set Print Area, Set Repeating Titles, Set Scale and Orientation, Set Sheet Print Options.

171

Print Workbook Data

The Print feature lets you print the current worksheet, a selection in a worksheet, or an entire workbook. Additionally, you can specify which pages to print, collate printed pages, print multiple copies, and print to a file.

Print button

Notes:

- Consider using **Print Preview** to check just how the worksheet will print prior to printing it *(see Print Preview).*

Settings that Affect Print Results

Before printing a worksheet or workbook, consider this checklist of settings that will affect the print results:

Headers and footers: Prints repeating information at the top and bottom of each page. *(See Headers and Footers.)*

Page breaks: Determines locations in worksheet where printed pages end and new pages start. *(See Page Breaks.)*

Margins: Determines free space around printed page. *(See Set Margins.)*

Orientation: Determines whether the page prints in a portrait or landscape orientation. *(See Set Scale and Page Orientation.)*

Print area: Prints a specified area of the worksheet. *(See Set Print Area.)*

Repeating print titles: Prints column titles at the top or left side of each new printed page. *(See Repeating Print Titles.)*

Scale: Determines the size of the worksheet information will be when printed. *(See Set Scale and Page Orientation.)*

Sheet options: Sets print options, such as gridlines, page order, draft quality, black and white printing. *(See Set Sheet Print Options.)*

Notes:

- Consider using **Print Preview** to check just how the worksheet will print prior to printing it *(see Print Preview).*

Print Using Toolbar

1 Select worksheets, worksheet cells, or chart object to print.
 OR
 Select any cell to print current worksheet.

2 Click **Print** button on Standard toolbar.

• In **step 1**, your selection will determine the parts of the workbook that you can print.

Print Using Menu

1 Select worksheets, worksheet cells, or chart object to print.

OR

Select any cell to print current worksheet.

2 Click **File** menu, then click **Print**.

The Print dialog box appears.

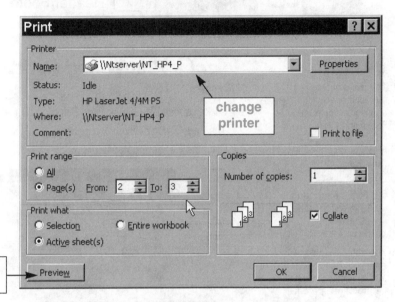

click to preview

To indicate what to print:

• Select **Selection**, **Entire workbook**, or **Active sheet(s)**.

To specify pages to print:

• Select **All**, or select pages to print in **From** and **To** boxes.

To disable collating of printed pages:

• Deselect **Collate**.

To print multiple copies:

• Select number of copies in **Number of copies** box.

To print to a file:

• Select **Print to file**.

3 Click **OK** to print.

Set Headers and Footers

Headers and footers are text that automatically repeat at the top and bottom of each page when you print. You can select predefined headers and footers or design your own.

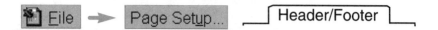

Notes:

- The margins and font size used will determine the number of lines you can include in your headers and footers *(see Margins)*.

- Excel maintains a separate header and footer for each worksheet. *(See TIP, below.)*

- You can preview how your headers and footers will look before printing *(see Print Preview)*.

Select a Predefined Header and Footer

1 Click **File** menu, then click **Page Setup**.

   The Page Setup dialog box appears.

2 Click the **Header/Footer** tab.

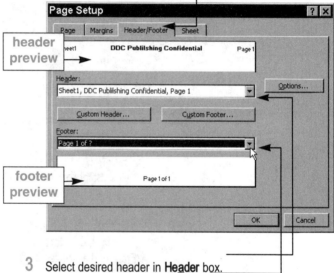

header preview

footer preview

3 Select desired header in **Header** box.

4 Select desired footer in **Footer** box.

5 Click **OK** when done.

> **TIP:** You can group worksheets (press Ctrl and click sheet tabs), then set the headers and footers for all selected sheets at one time.

Create a Custom Header and Footer

1 Click **File** menu, then click **Page Setup**.

The Page Setup dialog box appears.

2 Click the **Header/Footer** tab.

3 Click **Custom Header** or **Custom Footer**.

The Header or Footer dialog box appears.

4 Click in section to change.

5 Type or edit text.

To format text:

a Drag through text to format, then click the **Font** button.

b Select font option, then click **OK**.

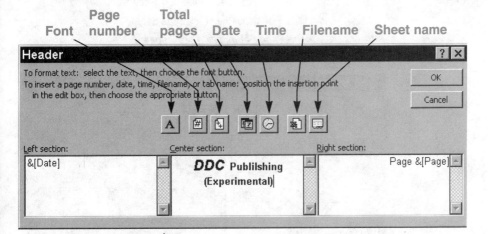

To insert a header or footer code:

a Place insertion point in section where code will be inserted.

b Click desired code button *(see Notes)*.

6 Click **OK** when done, then click **OK** to exit Page Setup.

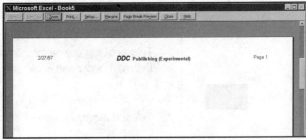

Result of Header Settings

Set Margins

Margins determine the amount of blank space between the printed contents of a page and the top, bottom, left and right edges of the page. Header and footer margins are measured from the top and bottom of the page, respectively.

📁 File ➡ Page Setup... ┌ Margins ┐

Notes:

- If your data does not fit within the margins, you can change the scale. (See Set Scale and Orientation.)

Set Page Margins from Page Setup

1 Select sheet or sheets to which you want margin settings to apply.

> NOTE: To select multiple sheets, press **Ctrl** and click each sheet tab you want to select.

2 Click **File** menu, then click **Page Setup**.

The Page Setup dialog box appears.

3 Click the **Margin** tab.

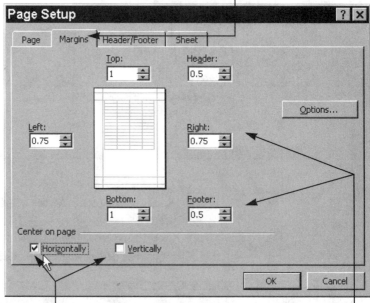

To set page margins:

- Type or select number of inches in **Top**, **Left**, **Right**, **Bottom**, **Header** and **Footer** margin boxes.

To center data within margins:

- Select **Horizontally** and/or **Vertically**.

- If your header margin is larger than the top margin, worksheet data and header information may overlap when you print. This note also applies to footers and the bottom margin.

Set Margins From Print Preview

For more information about Print Preview, see Print Preview.

1 Click **Print Preview button** on Standard toolbar.

2 Click **Margins** button on Print Preview toolbar.

   Margin and column handles appear in preview screen.

3 Drag margin handles to change their dimensions.

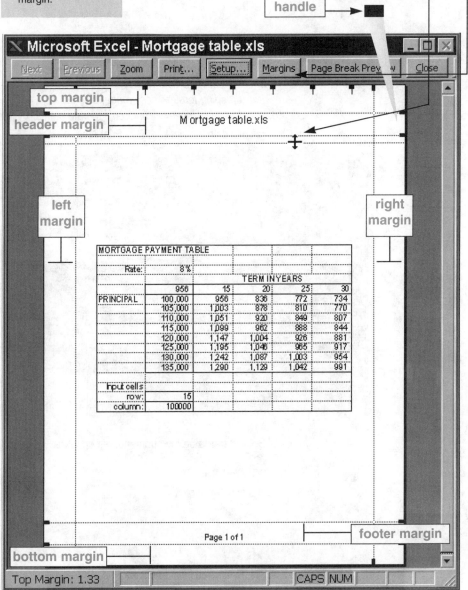

margin handle

top margin

header margin

Mortgage table.xls

left margin

right margin

MORTGAGE PAYMENT TABLE					
Rate:	8%				
			TERM IN YEARS		
	956	15	20	25	30
PRINCIPAL	100,000	956	836	772	734
	105,000	1,003	878	810	770
	110,000	1,051	920	849	807
	115,000	1,099	962	888	844
	120,000	1,147	1,004	926	881
	125,000	1,195	1,046	965	917
	130,000	1,242	1,087	1,003	954
	135,000	1,290	1,129	1,042	991
Input cells:					
row:	15				
column:	100000				

Microsoft Excel - Mortgage table.xls

Next | Previous | Zoom | Print... | Setup... | Margins | Page Break Preview | Close

Page 1 of 1

footer margin

bottom margin

Top Margin: 1.33   CAPS NUM

Set Print Area

Print area defines the range or ranges of a worksheet that will print when you issue a print command. If you select multiple ranges, each range will print on a separate page.

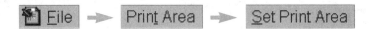

File ➡ **Print Area** ➡ **Set Print Area**

Set Print Area Using Menu

1 Select range or multiple ranges to print.

> *NOTE: To select multiple ranges, press **Ctrl** while dragging through each range to select. Multiple ranges will print on separate pages.*

2 Click **File** menu, then point to or click **Print Area**.

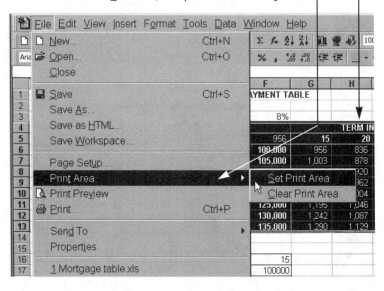

3 Click **Set Print Area** on the submenu that appears.

To change the print area:

• Repeat steps 1-3 above.

Clear a Print Area Using Menu

1 Click **File** menu, then point to or click **Print Area**.
2 Click **Clear Print Area** on the submenu that appears.

178

Set Print Area from Page Break Preview

In Page Break Preview, Excel highlights only the defined print areas in your worksheet. The remainder of the worksheet appears grey.

To open Page Break Preview:

FROM PRINT PREVIEW

• Click | Page Break Preview | on Page Preview toolbar.

FROM WORKSHEET

• Click **View** menu, then click **Page Break Preview**.

To set print area using shortcut menu:

a Select range of cells to print.

b Right-click selection.

   A shortcut menu appears.

c Click **Set Print Area**.

   Excel highlights only the defined print areas in your worksheet.

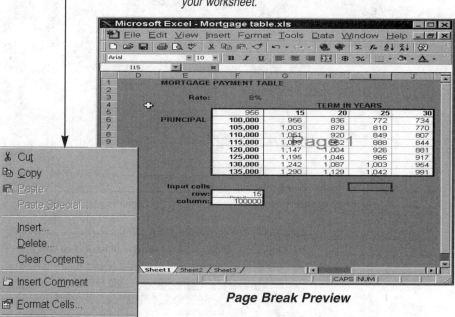

Page Break Preview

To add to print area using shortcut menu:

a Select additional ranges to print.

b Right-click selection.

   A shortcut menu appears.

c Click **Add to Print Area**.

   Excel highlights only the defined print areas in your worksheet.

print area options on shortcut menu

179

Set Repeating Print Titles

If you are printing a worksheet that spans many pages, you may want your row or column titles to appear on each printed page. You can set your worksheet to print in this manner from the Sheet tab on the Page Setup dialog box.

File ➡ Page Setup... | Sheet

Notes:

- After you set repeating rows and/or repeating columns, you can view the result before printing from Print Preview. *(See Print Preview.)*

- In most cases, you will set repeating rows or columns, but not both.

Set Titles of Worksheet Data to Print on Every Page

1 Click **File** menu, then click **Page Setup**.

The Page Setup dialog box appears.

2 Click the **Sheet** tab.

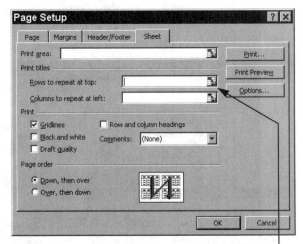

To set repeating row titles:

a Click in **Rows to repeat at top** box.

b Click the **Collapse Dialog** button on right side of box.

The dialog box collapses as shown below.

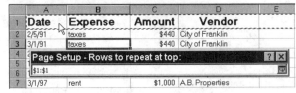

c In your worksheet, select rows containing titles to repeat when printing.

Excel inserts the row reference(s) in the box.

d Click the **Restore Dialog** button to restore dialog box to its previous size.

continued . . .

- If you access **Page Setup** from **Print Preview**, the **Sheet** options to set repeating rows and columns will not be available.

Set Titles of Worksheet Data to Print on Every Page (continued)

To set repeating column titles:

a   Click in **Columns to repeat at left** box.

b   Click the **Collapse Dialog** button on right side of box.

    The dialog box collapses as shown on left.

c   In your worksheet, select columns containing titles to repeat when printing.

    Excel inserts the column reference(s) in the box.

3   Click the **Restore Dialog** button to restore dialog box to its previous size.

4   Click **OK** when done.

5   Preview your worksheet *(see Print Preview)* to check the results.

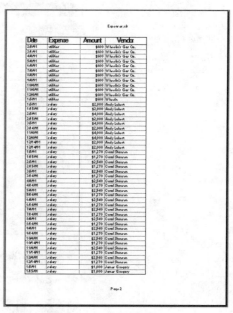

Page 1 and 2 with Repeating Row Titles

Set Scale and Orientation

Scale and Orientation are two page settings that determine your print results. Scaling lets you reduce or enlarge the printed contents, while Orientation lets you specify a portrait or landscape orientation for the printed page.

Notes:

- Before setting the scale to fit a large amount of data on one page, consider making the margins smaller *(See Set Margins)*. This will minimize the amount of scaling that needs to take place.

- Portrait orientation:

- Landscape orientation:

Set Scale, Orientation, and Related Page Settings

1 Click **File** menu, then click **Page Setup**.

The Page Setup dialog box appears.

2 Click the **Page** tab.

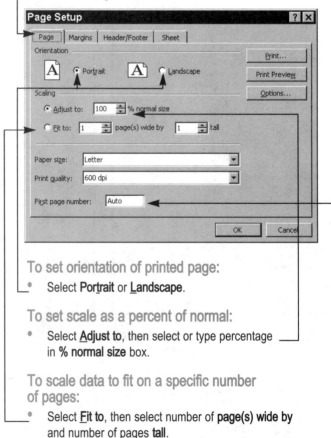

To set orientation of printed page:

- Select **Portrait** or **Landscape**.

To set scale as a percent of normal:

- Select **Adjust to**, then select or type percentage in **% normal size** box.

To scale data to fit on a specific number of pages:

- Select **Fit to**, then select number of **page(s) wide by** and number of pages **tall**.

To change the page number of first printed page:

- Type starting page number in **First page number** box.

182

Notes:

Notes:

- **Paper size** and **print quality** options will depend upon the capabilities of your installed printer.

To specify a paper size:

- Select paper size in **Paper si_z_e** list box.

To set print quality:

- Select desired print quality in **Print _q_uality** box.

3 Click **OK** when done.

normal scale with portrait orientation

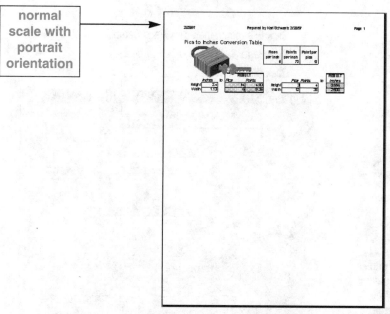

scale is 150% of normal with land-scape orientation

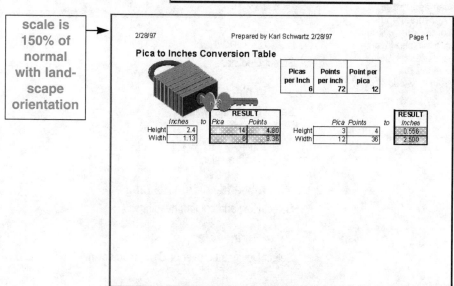

Scaling and Orientation Examples

Set Sheet Print Options

There are a variety of Sheet options you can set prior to printing your worksheet, including: gridlines, row and column headings, black and white printing, draft quality printing, printing comments, and the order of printing worksheets that print on multiple pages.

File → Page Setup... Sheet

Notes:

- **Print area** can be set from the **Sheet** tab or from the **File** menu *(see Set Print Area)*.

- For information about **Print titles** see *Set Repeating Print Titles*.

- The **Gridline** option does not affect how the gridlines appear on your worksheet on screen.

- You can select the **Black and white** option even if you have a color printer to reduce print time.

- Many sheet options, such as **Print area**, **Print titles**, and **Comments**, will not be available, if you access Page Setup from the Print Preview window.

Set Sheet Print Options

1 Click **File** menu, then click **Page Setup**.
   The Page Setup dialog box appears.

2 Click the **Sheet** tab.

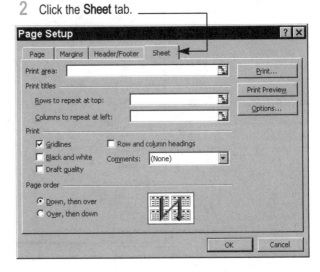

To print cell gridlines:
- Select **Gridlines**.

To print in black and white:
- Select **Black and white**.

To print in draft quality:
- Select **Draft quality**.

To print row and column headings:
- Select **Row and column headings**.

To set the print order:
- Select **Down, then over** or **Over, then down**.

continued . . .

Notes:

• For information about comments, see *Insert and Delete Comments.*

To print comments:

• Select **At end of sheet** or **As displayed on sheet** in **Comments** list box.

3 Click **OK** when done.

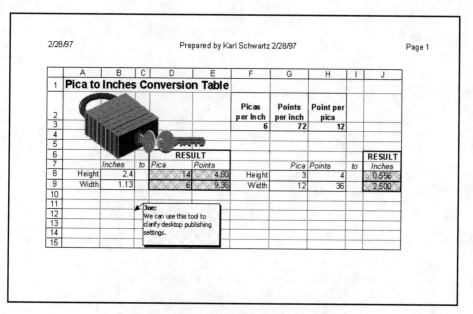

Sheet Options Include Gridlines, Comments, Row and Column Headings

Charts

This section contains illustrated procedures arranged in alphabetical order for creating and modifying charts.

About Chart Items

When you create and modify charts, you will be presented with many choices and settings. Understanding the items that make up a chart and their properties will make it easier for you to make decisions and to know what is possible.

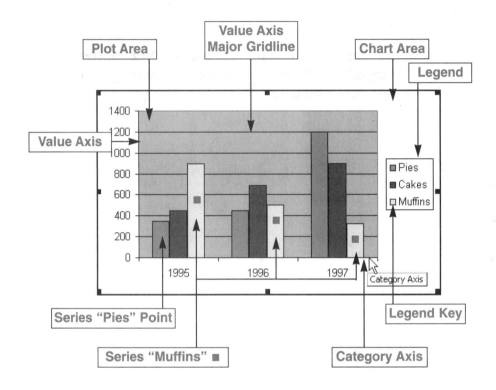

Items in Default Clustered Column Chart

Notes:

• When you rest the pointer on any chart item, Excel displays a pop-up label identifying the name of the item, as shown in the illustration (Category Axis) above.

Identify Chart Items

The default Clustered Column chart type shown above is made up of the items described below. Each item contains properties which are briefly described as well.

Category Axis (X Axis) — the horizontal line on which categories of data are usually plotted. The properties of this item include the format and alignment of category names and the scale of names and tick marks.

Chart Area — the space inside the chart that includes the base properties of all items in the chart, such as font style for chart text, background color, and how the chart moves or sizes when cells around it change.

- To review the properties of any chart item, rest the pointer on the item. When Excel displays the item name, double-click to display the Format dialog box for the item.

- Charts of different types have items or properties unique to their type. For example, pie charts have properties for a series that describes the angle of the first slice, while line charts have properties such as drop lines and up-down bars.

Legend — a box containing a label and legend key for each series in the chart. Properties of a legend include its border, font, and placement.

Legend Key — a graphic in the legend whose color or pattern corresponds to a series in the chart. Legend key properties include border, color, shadow, and fill effects.

Plot Area — the area within which the chart axes and series data is drawn. The properties of plot area include its border, area color, and fill effects.

Series — a group of data markers or series points that visually describe the values you have plotted. For example, the Series "Muffins" describes the number of muffins sold in each category (1995, 1996, and 1997). The properties of data series include borders and colors, plot axes, error bars, data labels, series order, and options such as overlap and gap width.

Series Point — a single item in a data series that visually describes the value for one category of a series. For example, Series "Pies" Point indicates a value of 345 for the category 1995. The properties for series points include border and pattern, data labels, and options such as overlap and gap width.

Value Axis (Y Axis) — the vertical line that describes the values of series points in the chart. The properties of the value axis include line and tick marks, scale of major and minor values, font for displayed values, number style of values, and alignment of values.

Value Axis Major Gridlines — a set of lines that visually defines values across the plot area. These gridlines make it easier to determine the value of a given series point in the chart. The properties of value axis gridlines include color, style, pattern, and units of values to display gridlines for.

Create a Chart

The Chart Wizard makes it easy to create a chart. It provides prompts and options for selecting the chart type, the source data, chart options, and chart location.

Chart Wizard button

Insert ➡ Chart...

Notes:

- The shape of your selection will determine the orientation of the series in your chart. You can change this orientation in **Chart Wizard - Step 2 of 4** in the **Data Range** tab.

- Avoid selecting blank rows and columns when selecting data to chart. You can use the **Ctrl** key and drag through ranges to create a multiple selection as a way to omit blank cells.

- You can hide rows and columns that do not pertain to data to be charted.

- From **Chart Wizard** steps, you can click **Next>** or **<Back** to move forward or backwards to any step.

- **Chart Wizard - Step 1 of 4:**

  First select the chart type, then the sub-type. You should click and hold the **Press and hold to view sample** button to preview how your chart will be plotted with the selected chart type.

Create a Chart

1 Select cells containing labels and values to chart.

    NOTE: *You can change this selection as you proceed, if you discover that your selection is not what was required to chart the data properly.*

2 Click **Chart Wizard** button on Standard toolbar.

From Chart Wizard - Step 1 of 4 - Chart Type:

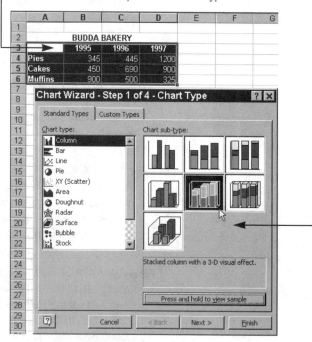

a Select chart type and subtype *(see Select Chart Type).*

b Click **Next >**.

continued . . .

- **Chart Wizard - Step 2 of 4:**

  From the **Data Range** tab, you can change the range of data to plot, or change the orientation of the data series to either columns or rows.

  From the **Series tab**, you can add and remove series and change references to series names, data ranges, and the category (X) axis labels.

From Chart Wizard - Step 2 of 4 - Chart Source Data:

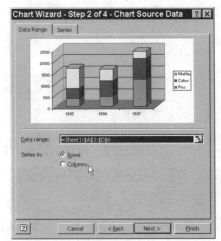

a   Select **Data Range** and **Series** options *(see Set Source of Chart Data).*

b   Click **Next >**.

From Chart Wizard - Step 3 of 4 - Chart Options:

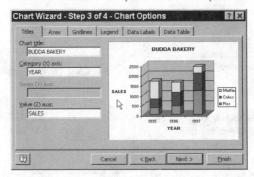

- **Chart Wizard - Step 3 of 4:**

  From the **Chart Options** dialog box, you can set options for chart titles, axes, gridlines, legend, data labels, and data table. You can go back to this dialog box after you've created the chart *(see Set Chart Options).*

a   Select desired **Chart** options *(See Set Chart Options).*

b   Click **Next >**.

From Chart Wizard - Step 4 of 4 - Chart Location:

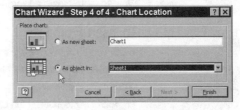

- **Chart Wizard - Step 4 of 4:**

  From the **Chart Location** dialog box, you can change the proposed destination sheet, or change the proposed chart sheet name.

  You can click **Finish** from any **Chart Wizard** step to quickly create the chart using default options.

a   Select **As new sheet** or **As object in** *(see Set Location of Chart).*

b   Click **Finish**.

Insert Objects in Charts

You can insert objects, such as picture files, AutoShapes, and WordArt, in your chart to add interest and bring attention to the information presented.

Notes:

- In **step 1**, you should select the chart prior to inserting the object, so the object moves and sizes with chart.

- Once an object is inserted in a chart, you can select and drag it to place it, or drag its sizing handles to change its size.

- After inserting multiple objects, you can change their order, so that one appears on top of another: Right-click the object, point to **Order** on the shortcut menu, then click desired order option such as **Bring to Front**.

- **From File option:** By default, the **Insert Picture** dialog box previews the selected picture file. From this dialog box, you can navigate folders as you would when opening or saving an Excel workbook.

  Excel accepts many graphic file formats including: JPG, JPEG, BMP, CDR, CGM, EPS, GIF.

Insert Objects in a Chart

1 Click the chart to select it.
OR
Select the chart sheet.

2 Click **Insert** menu, then point to or click **Picture**.

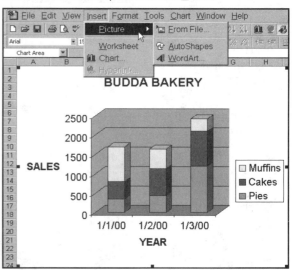

3 Click one of the following on the submenu that appears.
From File — to select a picture file stored on disk.
AutoShapes — to create an AutoShape object.
WordArt — to create a WordArt object.

To insert From File:

When you select this option the Insert Picture dialog box appears and provides tools for you to navigate folders and preview picture files.

- Select file to insert, then click **Insert** to place the picture in your chart.

continued . . .

- **AutoShapes option:**
  You can use tools on the Drawing toolbar to format objects drawn with tools on the AutoShapes toolbar.

- **WordArt options:**
  Consider using WordArt for text describing the chart title.

  You can use the tools on the WordArt toolbar to modify the object. For example, you can click the **Edit Text** button to change the text, or click the **Free Rotate** button to rotate the the WordArt object.

  Point to the objects on the WordArt toolbar to see the name of the button.

To insert AutoShapes:

When you select AutoShapes, the AutoShapes toolbar appears.

To display purpose of any button on toolbar:

- Rest pointer on toolbar button to identify.

To create an AutoShape object:

a Click desired button on the toolbar, then click desired shape on menu of shapes that appears.

b Drag through the chart area to draw the AutoShape object.

To insert WordArt :

When you select WordArt, Excel opens a WordArt Gallery dialog box.

a Click desired **WordArt** style in the list, then click **OK**.

b Type your text in the box provided, then select the font style for your text in the **Font** list box.

c Select the font size in the **Size** list box.

d Click **OK** to place the WordArt in the chart.

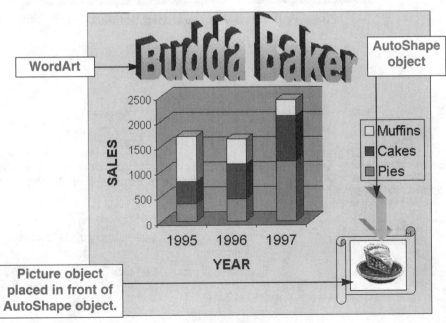

Chart with Objects

Format Chart Items

The appearance of every item in a chart can be changed or formatted. For example, you can change the border or color of the chart area, or fill a series with a blend effect or pictures stored in a graphic file on disk.

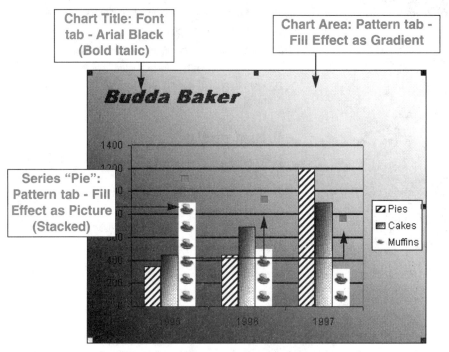

Chart Title: Font tab - Arial Black (Bold Italic)

Chart Area: Pattern tab - Fill Effect as Gradient

Series "Pie": Pattern tab - Fill Effect as Picture (Stacked)

Items Formatted in a Clustered Column Chart

Notes:

- When you rest the pointer on any chart item, Excel displays a pop-up label identifying the name of the item as shown in the illustration (Category Axis) above.

Format Chart Items

This is a list of format options for each chart item in the default Clustered Column chart type. Format options may vary for different chart types.

1 Double-click the chart item to format.

2 Select the tab containing the category of the format you want to change.

3 Select desired options, then click **OK**.

- See *About Chart Items* to see an illustration of the chart items listed here.

- Charts of different types will have items or properties unique to their type. For example, pie charts will have properties for a series that describes the angle of the first slice, while line charts will have properties such as drop lines and up-down bars.

Format Options for Chart Items

Category Axis (X Axis)

Patterns style of line and tick marks, **Scale** of axis and categories, **Font** style of category labels, **Number** style of category labels, **Alignment** of category labels.

Chart Area

Patterns style of area—shadow, round corners, area color, fill effects (gradient, texture, pattern, picture); **Font** style of text (base font for chart).

Legend

Patterns style of area—border, shadow, area color, fill effects (gradient, texture, pattern, picture); **Font** style of text; **Placement** of legend in chart.

Legend Key

Patterns style of area—shadow, round corners, area color, fill effects (gradient, texture, pattern, picture).

Plot Area

Patterns style of border, area color, fill effects (gradient, texture, pattern, picture).

Series

Patterns style of border, shadow, and area—color and fill effects (gradient, texture, pattern, picture); **Axis** series on primary or secondary axis; **Y Error Bars** style and criteria, **Data Labels** options; **Series Order**; **Options** specific to chart type.

Series Point

Patterns style of border, shadow, and area—color, fill effects (gradient, texture, pattern, picture); **Data Labels** options; **Options** specific to chart type.

Value Axis (Y Axis)

Patterns style of axis line; **Scale** of axis and categories; **Font** style category labels; **Number** style of category labels; **Alignment** of category labels.

Value Axis Major Gridlines

Patterns style of gridlines; **Scale** of major and minor gridlines.

Move and Size Chart Items

Charts are composed of items such as the Chart Area and the Plot area *(see About Chart Items)*. After you create a chart you can position and size these items to present the chart data as you like it.

Notes:

- In **step 1**, when you rest the mouse pointer on an item, Excel displays a pop-up label that identifies the item name, as shown in illustration on the right (Plot Area).

Move and Size a Chart Item

1 Rest your pointer on the item to identify it.
2 Click the item to select it.

An outline and sizing handles appear around item.

item border

sizing handles

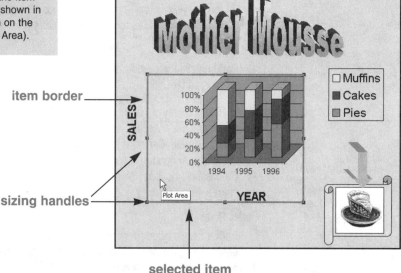

selected item

To size selected item:

- Drag sizing handle in direction to size the item

As you the drag sizing handle, a dashed border indicates the new shape of the item.

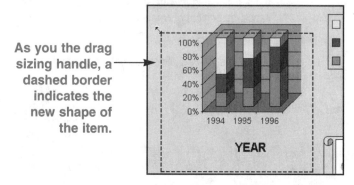

196

continued . . .

- Some items, such as axis labels, must be moved by dragging the border. Clicking inside these items allows you to edit the text.

- Some items, such as Category and Value Axes, cannot be moved and sized directly. These items will change size as you change the size of the **Plot Area**.

- You can size and move the entire chart by dragging the sizing handles when the **Chart Area** is selected.

Move and Size a Chart Item (continued)

To move selected item:

- Drag border or empty area of selected item in direction to move the item.

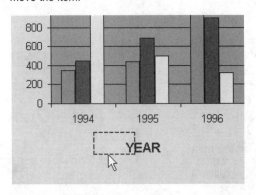

Excel displays the border of item as you drag it.

Chart Area sizing handles

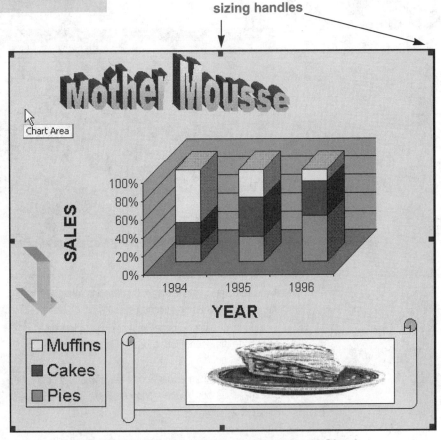

Original Chart with Items Moved and Sized

Print Charts

You can print a chart as part of a worksheet *(see Print a Worksheet)* or print it as a separate item on a page. Prior to printing a chart, you can set options to control the size and position of the chart on the printed page.

Notes:

- In **step 1**, if you do not select the chart in the worksheet, you will not be able to print the chart apart from the worksheet data.

- Chart sheet tabs appear along the bottom of the workbook with the sheet tabs.

Set Page Options for Printing Chart Only

1   Click the chart to print in worksheet.

   OR

   Click chart sheet tab.

2   Click **File** menu, then click **Page Setup**.

   The Page Setup dialog box appears.

3   Click the **Chart** tab. _____

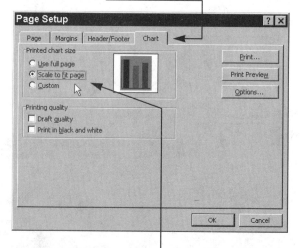

4   Select a printed chart size. _____

5   If you selected **Custom**, select the **Margins** tab to set margins and centering options.

6   By default, charts are printed in landscape orientation. To change the orientation, click the **Page** tab and select the **Portrait** option.

7   If desired, click the **Header/Footer** tab and select or create a header *(see Set Headers and Footers)*.

8   Click **OK** when done.

Notes:

- From Print Preview, you can set margins and access the **Page Setup** dialog box to change page options *(see Print Preview)*.

Preview Chart

1 Click the chart to print in worksheet.

   OR

   Click desired chart sheet tab.

2 Set page options as described on previous page.

   FROM PAGE SETUP DIALOG BOX:

   - Click Print Preview

   OR

   FROM WORKSHEET OR CHART SHEET:

   - Click **Print Preview button** on Standard toolbar.

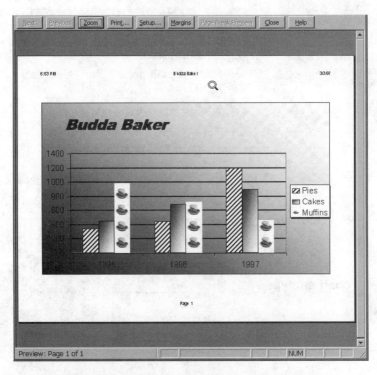

Preview of Chart with Header and Footer

Notes:

- You can also print the chart from Print Preview *(see Print Preview)*.

Print Chart

1 Click the chart to print in worksheet.

   OR

   Click chart sheet tab.

2 Set page options as described on previous page.

3 Click **Print button** on Standard toolbar.

Select Chart Type

Excel provides 14 standard chart types, such as Area, Column, and Pie charts. Each chart type contains a variety of subtypes, such as Pie with 3-D visual effect. In addition to standard chart types, you can choose from many custom types or define your own.

Chart Wizard button

Notes:

- Choosing a chart type is a lot like trying on clothes that you intend to buy in a department store, except that it's faster and easier to do.

Select a Chart Type

When charting data, you should keep in mind the kind of data you are plotting and the purpose of the chart. With Chart Wizard, it is easier than ever to make a good decision about the chart type because you can view a sample of your chart without leaving the dialog box.

1 Follow steps to create a chart *(see Create a Chart).*

OR

- Select chart or chart sheet.
- Click **Chart** menu, then **Chart Type**.

The Chart Type dialog box appears.

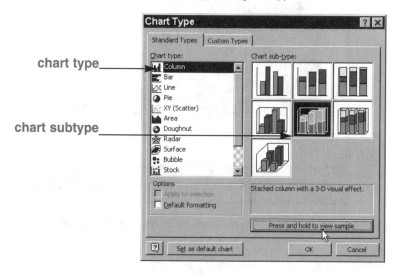

2 Click the **Standard** tab and select desired chart type in **Chart type** list.

Excel displays subtypes in Chart sub-type list.

3 Click the desired chart subtype in **Chart sub-type** list.

continued . . .

Notes:

- To create a chart you have formatted to the **User-defined** list, format the chart: Click **Chart** menu, then **Chart Type**, click the **Custom** tab, select **User-defined**, then click **Add**.

4 Click and hold mouse button down on **Press and hold to view sample** button to preview a sample of your chart with selected chart type.

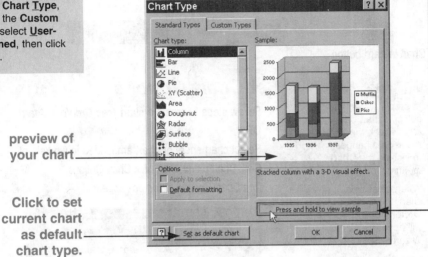

preview of your chart

Click to set current chart as default chart type.

To set current selection as default chart type:

- Click **Set as default chart**.

To select a custom chart type:

- Click the **Custom Types** tab, then select desired chart type in **Chart type** list.

  Excel displays Sample in Sample box.

Click to display custom charts you have defined.

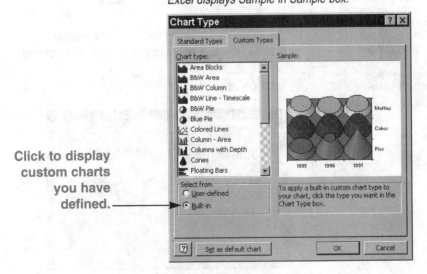

5 Click **OK** or **Finish** when done.

Set Chart Options

The Chart Wizard provides the Chart Options dialog box, where you can select from an array of chart options. As you make your selections, the Chart Wizard shows you the results in a sample box — making this feature a great learning tool. After you create the chart, you can access this same dialog box to change options at a later time.

Chart Wizard button

Notes:

- In **step 1**, when you select a chart or chart sheet, the menu bar changes to include the **Chart** menu option.

- When creating a chart, the **Chart Options** dialog box will appear in Chart Wizard - Step 3 of 4.

- [?] If you want to know the purpose of any setting, click the question mark button, then click the option. A pop-up window will appear to describe it.

- Chart options depend on the chart type. For example, Pie charts will have only three category tabs:
Titles, **Legend**, and **Data Labels**.

Set Chart Options

1 Follow steps to create a chart *(see Create a Chart)*.
OR
Select chart sheet or chart embedded in worksheet.

2 Click **Chart** menu, then click **Chart Options**.
The Chart Options dialog box appears.

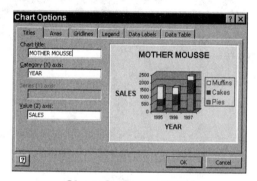

Chart Options: Titles

3 Select the tab containing the option category you want to change, then select options appropriate to your chart type.

4 Click **OK** when done.

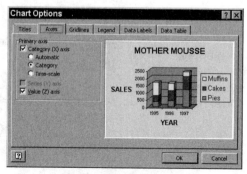

Chart Options: Axes

continued . . .

Notes:

- Don't hesitate to try a setting. Excel will display the result in the sample box. If it is not what you want, just remove it.

- If you add an item (such as a data table) to your chart, but the item does not fit well within the chart area, you can still accept the option and size or set the position of the item (or surrounding items) later on *(see Move and Size Chart Items)*.

- When you add items to a chart (such as Chart titles, and data tables), you do not have to accept the initial format. When you return to the chart, double-click the item to open a Format dialog box specific to the item *(see Format Chart Items)*.

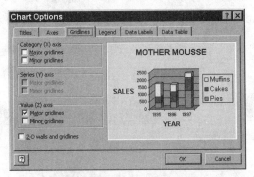

Chart Options: Gridlines

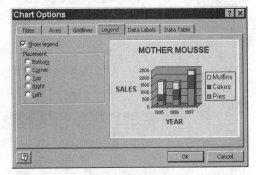

Chart Options: Legend

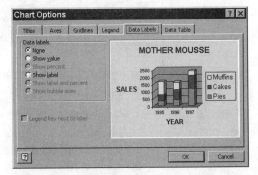

Chart Options: Data Labels

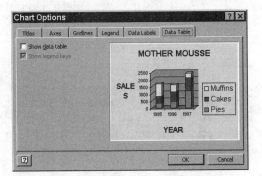

Chart Options: Data Table

Set Location of Chart

The Chart Location dialog box lets you set the location of a new chart or change the location of an existing chart. If the destination is a chart sheet, Excel lets you name the sheet. If the destination is a worksheet, you must select the sheet from a list of existing sheet names.

Chart Wizard button

Notes:

* If you want a chart in both locations, you can copy the sheet containing the chart, then change the location of the chart on the copied sheet *(see Sheet Tabs)*.

Set Location of Chart

1　Follow steps to create a chart *(see Create a Chart)*, and proceed to *Chart Wizard - Step 4 of 4 - Chart Location*.

OR

* Select existing chart or chart sheet.
* Click **Chart** menu, then **Location**.

The Chart Location dialog box appears.

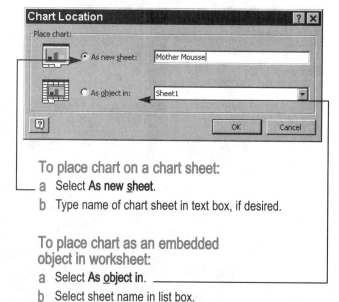

To place chart on a chart sheet:
a　Select **As new sheet**.
b　Type name of chart sheet in text box, if desired.

To place chart as an embedded object in worksheet:
a　Select **As object in**.
b　Select sheet name in list box.

2　Click **OK** when done.

continued . . .

TIP:　Although chart sheets do not automatically show worksheet data, you may include it in the chart by setting the chart option to Show data table *(see Set Chart Options)*.

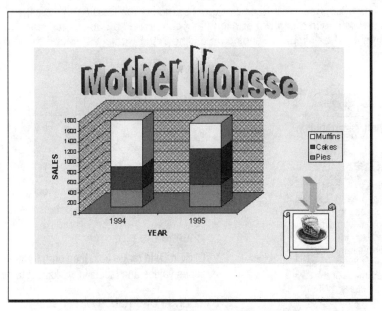

Printed Chart on Chart Sheet

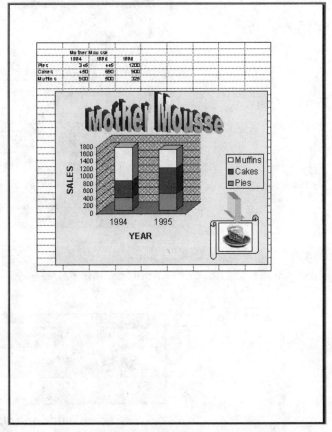

Printed Chart as Object on Worksheet

Set Source of Chart Data

Excel provides new tools to help you set or modify the location of worksheet data that you are plotting in a chart. For example, you can add an additional year of data to an existing chart by simply extending an outline in the worksheet data with the mouse.

Chart Wizard button

Chart ➜ Source Data...

Notes:

- When changing the plot area, Excel will collapse the dialog box as you drag through the data range in the worksheet, so you can see more of the worksheet. When you complete the selection, Excel returns the dialog box to its normal size.

Set Source Data Using Menu

1 Select chart in worksheet or chart sheet.
2 Click **Chart** menu, then **Source Data**.

To change the plot area:

- Click in **Data range** box, then drag through series values and labels in worksheet to plot.

To change orientation of series:

- Select Series in **Rows** or **Columns**.

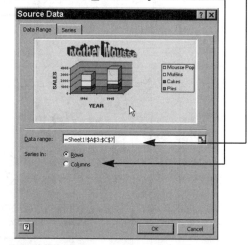

TIP: You can add, remove, and define individual series from the Series tab in the Source Data dialog box.

references for **Name** and **Values** for selected series

selected series

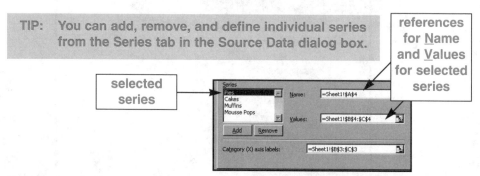

Series Tab: Controls

Set Source Location of Chart Data Using Mouse

You can only use this procedure for a chart embedded in a worksheet.

- Select **Chart Area** of chart.

  Excel marks plotted data area in worksheet with borders and extend handles.

border of category labels

border of chart series

extend handles

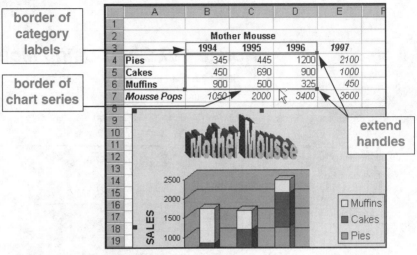

To change cells plotted by chart:

- Drag border that surrounds plotted worksheet values to desired location.

New series plotted: Cakes, Muffins, and Mousse Pops.

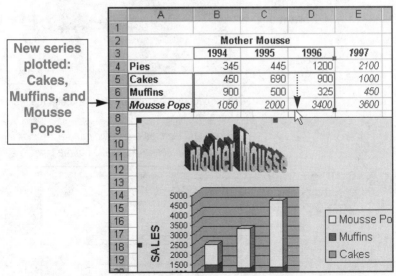

To change range of cells plotted by chart:

- Drag extend handle of border that surrounds values or category to include or exclude data.

Special 3-D Chart Effects

After you create a 3-D chart *(see Set Chart Type)*, you can adjust the view of the chart interactively, or by changing rotation and elevation settings in a dialog box.

Notes:

- To create a 3-D chart see *Set Chart Type*.

- In **step 3**, you can rest pointer on any chart item to identify its name.

- You can click **Edit** menu, then **Undo 3-D View** to undo the rotation of the chart.

Rotate 3-D Chart Using Mouse

1 Select the chart in worksheet or chart sheet.

2 Click inside walls of chart.

Corner handles appear around the chart's 3-dimensional space.

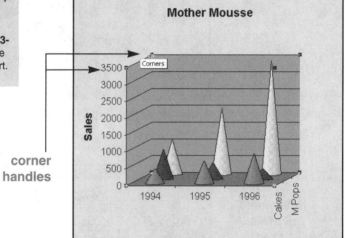

corner handles

3 Drag any corner handle to rotate and change the elevation of the chart.

The pointer becomes a crosshair and a 3-D box indicates the current rotation and elevation of the chart.

Drag corner to change 3-D view.

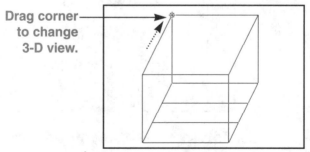

4 Release mouse button to accept the rotation and elevation indicated by 3-D outline.

Notes:

- Other 3-D View options:

  Auto scaling — scale a 3-D chart to be closer in size to the 2-D version. This setting is available only when **Right angle axes** is selected.

  Right angle axes — deselect to free the chart from the right angle constraint. Excel will enable a Perspective setting, and buttons will appear to let you change the perspective with the mouse.

  Height % of base — type a percentage to control height in relation to length of x axis. This setting is available only when **Right angle axes** is deselected.

  Default — click to return chart to its default 3-D settings.

Rotate 3-D Chart Using Dialog Box Commands

1 Select the chart in worksheet or chart sheet.

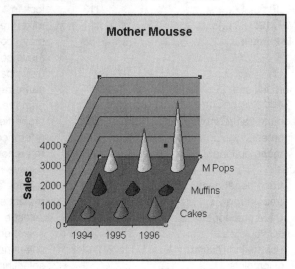

2 Click **Chart** menu, then **3-D View**.
   The 3-D View dialog box appears.

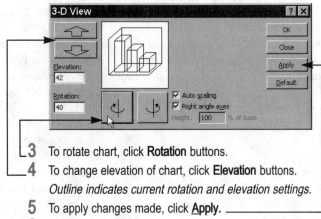

3 To rotate chart, click **Rotation** buttons.

4 To change elevation of chart, click **Elevation** buttons.
   Outline indicates current rotation and elevation settings.

5 To apply changes made, click **Apply**.

6 Click **OK** when done.

209

Index

215

More Fast-teach Learning Books

Did we make one for you?

Title	Cat. No.
Corel WordPerfect 7 for Win 95	Z12
DOS 5–6.2 (Book & Disk)	D9
DOS + Windows	Z7
Excel 5 for Windows	E9
Excel 7 for Windows 95	XL7
INTERNET	Z15
Lotus 1-2-3 Rel. 2.2–4.0 for DOS	L9
Lotus 1-2-3 Rel. 4 & 5 for Windows	B9
Microsoft Office	M9
Microsoft Office for Windows 95	Z6
Windows 3.1 – A Quick Study	WQS-1
Windows 95	Z3
Word 2 for Windows	K9
Word 6 for Windows	1-WDW6
Word 7 for Windows 95	Z10
WordPerfect 5.0 & 5.1 for DOS	W9
WordPerfect 6 for DOS	P9
WordPerfect 6 for Windows	Z9
WordPerfect 6.1 for Windows	H9
Works 3 for Windows	1-WKW3
Works 4 for Windows 95	Z8

DESKTOP PUBLISHING LEARNING BOOKS	
Word 6 for Windows	Z2
WordPerfect 5.1 for DOS	WDB
WordPerfect 6 for Windows	F9
WordPerfect 6.1 for Windows	Z5